THE BACK HOME SERIES

Praise for
The Long Fields

"If you want to know what it's like to grow up on a large Michigan family farm, if you want to study deep into the fields, the animals, the turning of the fall maples, if you want to find where the morel mushrooms hide, if you want to watch the strands of a beloved blue sweater unravel into the wind to nurture everything in sight, Anne-Marie Oomen's glorious essays will give you all that. What else they'll give you is intensely personal: the necessary tension of a writer as she steps back, pushes against the beloved soil that nurtured her, but can't completely leave it behind."

—Fleda Brown
Poet Laureate of Delaware
author of *Mortality, With Friends*

"With such a fine chemistry of poetry, prose and even brilliant reporting, Anne-Marie Oomen takes us beautifully and startlingly up close to the details of life, and then transports us to places sometimes wonderful and sometimes dark in our own hearts and minds and worlds."

—Jeff Smith
author of *Becoming Amish*

"If Michigan had its own distinct literary footprint, its terroir, I think Anne-Marie Oomen's essays would be featured prominently on the menu. Her words and stories walk us through Michigan's seasons, our relationship with the land, and how this place defines us. I'll pick up *The Long Fields* when I crunch into my first raw asparagus spear in May, and again with the August sweetcorn, and again when canned fruits are exchanged as gifts near a roaring fire during the winter season."

—Jacob Wheeler
author of *Angel of the Garbage Dump*

"This book is stunning. With its compassion, reflection, and celebration, Anne-Marie Oomen's *The Long Fields* offers us a balm for our too-often battered hearts. In prose both lyrical and accessible, Oomen explores the idea of 'homing,' the process— she tells us—of making a home. Here is a home remembered, another built, and still others found and made in her relationships to and love of family, friends, lovers, ritual, and this precious land. Oomen's essays are like an open invitation to step inside these pages, to find a place to settle, and to make ourselves at home."

—Patricia Ann McNair
author of *Responsible Adults* and *Temple of Air*

Anne-Marie Oomen

The Long Fields

Essays of Home and Comfort

CORNERSTONE PRESS
UNIVERSITY OF WISCONSIN-STEVENS POINT

Cornerstone Press, Stevens Point, Wisconsin 54481
Copyright © 2023 Anne-Marie Oomen
www.uwsp.edu/cornerstone

Printed in the United States of America by
Point Print and Design Studio, Stevens Point, Wisconsin

Library of Congress Control Number: 2023933430
ISBN: 978-1-960329-99-8

This is a work of creative nonfiction. All of the events in this book are true to the best of the author's memory. Some names and identifying features have been changed to protect the identity of certain parties. The author in no way represents any company, corporation, or brand, mentioned herein. The views expressed in this memoir are solely those of the author.

Cornerstone Press titles are produced in courses and internships offered by the Department of English at the University of Wisconsin–Stevens Point.

DIRECTOR & PUBLISHER   EXECUTIVE EDITOR
Dr. Ross K. Tangedal   Jeff Snowbarger

SENIOR EDITORS
Lexie Neeley, Monica Swinick, Kala Buttke

PRESS STAFF
Ellie Atkinson, Lauren Engelbreth, Hannah Fenrick, Patrick Fogarty, Angela Green, Cal Henkens, Brett Hill, Julia Kaufman, Catriona Scheinost, Maria Scherer, Cash Van Stiphout, Matt Vancik, Abbi Wasielewski

To the story-tellers and poem-sayers, all, wherever you are, but especially to the Beach Bards, our Leelanau County storytelling group that has kept poetry and narrative vital on summer Fridays in Leelanau for over thirty years: Norm Wheeler, Bronwyn Jones, Joe VanderMuelen, "Fuzz," and our supportive spouses, Mimi Wheeler and David Early.

And to the early practitioners from whom we learned to circle a fire and speak the old way: Max Ellison, Terry Wooten, Taelen Thomas, Luanne Lechler, Ray Nargis, John Kelly, and Frank Ettawagezic.

Also by Anne-Marie Oomen:

NONFICTION

As Long As I Know You: The Mom Book

Love, Sex, and 4H: A Memoir

An American Map: Essays

House of Fields: Memories of a Rural Education

Pulling Down the Barn: Memories of a Rural Childhood

POETRY

The Lake Michigan Mermaid (with Linda Nemec Foster)

Uncoded Woman: Poems

Moniker (with R.E. Nargis)

EDITED COLLECTIONS

Elemental: A Collection of Michigan Nonfiction

Looking Over My Shoulder: Reflections on the Twentieth Century

Contents

Part III: Kuieren

Author's Note

The Long Fields is a retrospective of essays I wrote about home and land over several decades, those places where I grew up and the places where my husband and I built our home. It includes dozens of previously published and collected pieces from over the years along with a few new ones. (Yikes, I'm too young for a "new and collected," aren't I? Ahem.) Today some of these essays seem almost historical documents, and now I need to examine that potentially nostalgic view. At the time I wrote them, I overlooked the much earlier stewardship of land by the indigenous people of this region of Michigan. Because many of these pieces grew from my earliest writing days when I was still claiming the moniker of writer and still uncertain of my younger heart or my subject, I was sometimes writing from inside a naïve narrative. Many of these pieces are columns written for magazines or periodicals to honor Michigan's rural culture as I experienced it, and many were limited by a word count that kept them both short and uncomplicated. I am now aware of the much longer history that exists in this region and that I here humbly acknowledge. The site where we built a house and gardens was home to an ancient and present people who I hold in gratitude. When I place my feet where earlier people walked, hunted, lived, and still live, I try now to be attentive to the longer field of history—the people who once tended and stewarded the land. To be more specific, this region, Northwestern Lower Michigan, is the ancestral lands of the Anishinaabe people of the Three Fires Confederacy of the Ojibwe, Ottawa, and Potawatomi peoples who are today represented by the nations of the Grand Traverse Band of Ottawa and Chippewa Indians and the Little Traverse Bay Bands of Odawa Indians. I thank them for their past efforts on behalf of the land and for their continued presence.

Though only a few essays address that history directly, I hope place-love and earth-respect rise as dominant themes. From those themes, a homing that I had not expected. Of the newer essays, I wrote again about the process of making a home, not to be confused with home-making in the old school sense. Also, for the first time are essays about the courtship between my husband David and me, and about how we built our handmade house. I am grateful to David for the careful way he guided us in building so much of the house from recycled materials, and for helping to build the gardens that have raised some of our food and restored a tiny fraction of the soil. But for a long time, we remained uncertain about the larger acreage—how best to honor the soil, and offer respect to those first stewards. The acreage we walk has been abused by decades of exposure to chemicals and orchard practices that damaged the soil. I kept asking how to do that. Then two years ago, I was given a plug of native sweet grass—a plant that is held sacred by many indigenous people. I transplanted it to a pot, and a year later, replanted the root mass into a small bed that can be protected. I understood that if I could keep it moist and healthy enough, it would discourage the wind erosion of our sandy soil and further deter invasives—being a hearty spreader itself. Just days before this introduction was completed, that sweet grass blossomed for the first time. Growing sweet grass is not justice, but it brings hope for the soil. I acknowledge that this is an empty gesture if not accompanied by a more concrete action. I am seeking that direction with each blade I touch and with the new words I write.

I am also grateful to those who first published these pieces, for that opportunity was also a gift. These are listed more extensively at the end of this book. But here let me acknowledge that none of this collection would be possible without Cornerstone Press, particularly director Dr. Ross Tangedal, along with Maria Scherer, Brett Hill, and all the editors and wonder workers at the press. Again, my sincerest gratitude.

For those who would like to learn more about the indigenous people of Northwestern Lower Michigan, please explore the following sites:

https://ltbbodawa-nsn.gov/
https://www.gtbindians.org/membership.asp

To support change and to donate in support of indigenous learners, join this fund:

https://engage.collegefund.org/page/22097/donate/1

AMO

Prologue: The Long Fields

There's a certain slant of light
Winter afternoons—
That oppresses, like the heft
Of cathedral tunes—

Heavenly hurt, it gives us—
We find no scar
But internal difference,
Where the meanings, are—

                               —Emily Dickinson

When it is too cold to walk out alone, I walk out alone, out of the woods and into an open field south of our home in the wooded hills just east of the tiny village of Empire, Michigan. I am worried—my stepson, my colleagues at work, my parents, the world as it is. I am carrying beeswax candles to the neighbors. I do this for the winter solstice. I should stay on the narrow, single-plowed roads, should walk between the banks to these distant homes whose lights haze through the snow in blurry squares, but instead, I climb over those rough boundaries out into the long field, into the wind and snow to trudge cross country through weed stubble and the strata of powder deep enough to cake around the tops of my Sorrels.

It takes a while to cross a snow-covered field, and there is time to think.

I feel old winter, the one I know in my hands and thighs and long dreams, the one of my life. I move with the wind, with the force of invisible and precious cold which is always at the center of everything winter. In the southwest sky, low sun shifts lower. The light changes, turns golden when it should be blue. Lake effect clouds color up with rose. I stop. There it is—the clean sweep, the view at dusk, the hard walk, the buried danger or sorrow.

The look at the interior, the full length of it. The look is inside at the same time.

In all its austere beauty, winter is still loneliness, the loneliness of being one, a separate being, an original curse or gift, with and not with. And it comes to me: we are one long wind over long fields, pushing over a still and quiet land as we move from one end to the other where finally, the old tree line protects us.

Here on the edge of a long field, we can look back at the stubble and the empty rows, the places where the corn grew, the wheat was sheared, the carrots were pulled, and here too is where time unfolds backwards, like a curve of the cosmos. I stand in a wind not of this world, looking at the footprints, seeing the tiny bits of wonder with each step, connecting these to the past, the row or path I followed all the way back. Here, here, here is where this happened.

Part I

Childhood's Lamplight

As a child I thought language made a bubble in which you could survive. A weightless stillness, a clearing—something, anyway: a wake in the unnamable dark. I was the girl writing alone in the lamplight, unschooled, seizing at something that wouldn't stop leaping, that kept changing shape.

—Melita Schaum, Sinner of Memory

Head Cheese

If you have not yet realized that hunger begins with death, skip this essay. Because butchering is its own story and you need to finish what you start. I promise that elsewhere in this book there is lightness, elsewhere a ridiculous amount of hope, tenderness, even sentiment. Peonies, sweet grapes. The scent of cucumber. But if you can bear an old-school truth that has much to do with survival, read on. Still, a warning.

This is also about writing, how I write, how I will tell the stories.

My father has placed the eight-pound pig's head on his workbench in the basement. He takes the hacksaw from the nail on the two-by-four stud next to the stairs and forces the blade between the gleaming teeth at the back of the jaw. Once positioned, he uses one hand to brace it and saws through the jaw to separate it and the tongue from the main head. He has already cut off the ears. They rest to the side, stiff, almost plastic in their perfect formation, like flesh leaves. The pig's head slips around and nearly slides off the bench, so I step forward, placing my hands on the head, holding it against the rasp of his sawing motion. I can feel the vibration of the saw against the jaw, the way each tooth of sharpened metal tears the bone.

I am now part of the story. I am participating. I am also home in Oceana County for a few brief days before returning to teaching. But here, I am holding tight to the pig's head. He is doing this on my account. My mother had given me the new parish cookbook. The book includes reprints of classic "homespun" recipes along with new recipes added by the younger women who weren't cooking ten years ago. In my mother's plain, direct prose, I am shocked to find a description of butchering a pig. She writes dispassionately about the scalding pots, cutting bones, and head cheese.

"Head cheese? What's that?"

"Oh, we cooked the head down and then stripped off the meat and fat and gristle, and well, it's all kind of jelly-like, and chilled up, it slices like bologna, for sandwiches. Gramma's was very good; it was considered a delicacy." She looks embarrassed again. Often the practices of her youth embarrass her.

"You cooked the pig's head?" I'm aghast. I'm fascinated.

"We used everything." She looks at me with quiet tolerance.

"Everything but the squeal," my father adds, grinning.

I want the recipe.

She doesn't have it. "We just did it. Made it."

I ask how it was done, and they say they can't remember, but as my parents speak back and forth, it returns like a dove to the loft, this way of living. They do remember what they did and how it was to be cooked, and finally they talk themselves into it. They will show me. They will tell the head cheese story. My mother calls two butchers before she finds one who has a hog's head in his freezer—the brains removed already, but that was all, so *pretty authentic*, she says. The head is empty of brains?

Head cheese is a process that begins with removing the thinking parts.

I am the collector of stories in this now fourth generation American family of Dutch-Belgian descent. Much of my writing has sprung from incidents I have gathered, from oral history told casually around supper tables and over morning coffee. I am not a purist and certainly not an archivist. I rarely use a tape recorder, and though I often take notes, I am transposing my own vision over the tale even as it is spoken. It is raw material. It is something of the mind and body, not history. It is honoring the presence in physical life—the quotidian stuff of being, and from that, I stir a story.

I do this because I am a writer and because what my family says often is not yet story. In their rough flannels and jeans and broken-soled boots and Carhartts, they do not perceive themselves as tellers. They shrug, tell truncated versions without much life. However, if I can tie an anecdote to work, to some activity—from hoeing the garden to making soup, they do not have to look at me. They can move their hands in a task; then the story rises. Ask my mother to tell a story of courtship, a travel adventure, or a family tragedy and she will say, "It was nothing much." Ask her how to milk a cow, set a hen, make sweet pickles hold their color (green food coloring!) and she can tell you to the minutest detail, adding variations learned from other practitioners. "Your aunt didn't do it this way. She used a pressure cooker. It's faster but it exploded once, that's how she got burned, you know those scars on her arms, always in a hurry. I like the slow cook way." And if you stay quiet or ask small questions—you get a kind of plot to work. Sometimes you learn character, the themes of their lives: frugality, survival, resilience, and toughness in the instructions. Epiphany. Head cheese. That recipe.

My father's saw crunches through the back jaw of the pig's head. Bits of tissue scatter the workbench. Now the jaw, with its broken teeth gleaming, lies open and its tongue, utterly surprising, no longer screams in the sty. The upper skull, earless, still has eyes of sorts—its irises are freezer-burned gray-blue, staring blankly at the light bulb dangling from the ceiling. My father attacks these next.

"We always took these out," he says. "Don't know if you need to, but there might have been a good reason." He will remove the eyes? He will blind a creature that already cannot see? Yes, I think. The dead do not see the way we do.

Taking the small sharp jackknife that is his trademark, he cuts the gristle around the eye. There is no fluid, but the main nerve is tough and even with his knife, he can't cut the fiber that once fed these eyes with the sight of slop being poured, rain to soften the dirt and create their beloved mud, all the pig needed to move around in the pen, to find the mash and water troughs. Dad asks for another knife with a longer blade and finally asks for the pliers. Geeze. He grabs the eye just under the ball and pulls it out, using the knife to cut the stretch of muscle as he pulls. I turn away for a moment and swallow. Maybe this story is like so many remnants of our lives, too violent to comprehend. Or maybe this is where the stories really live, when they become too hard to view. I make myself turn back, become a part of what kept people alive, the brutal sacrifice of the animal for the necessity cooked to delicacy.

My mother remembers, "After all the preparations, and we were ready, I was sent to my room until the pigs were dead."

This is a surprise. "Why, mom, I saw you butcher chickens when I was a kid." More than that if I counted the hand-butchering she did in deer season. I thought the butchering was communal, including the women.

"I guess women weren't supposed to see these big animals die—especially if someone was pregnant. Not the death. The men didn't want us upset—we were often the ones who knew the creature best, who did the raising up, the feeding. But once the animals were dead and blooded, we handled every ounce of the meat." Here is a part of the story I never would have found, that even in that rough and tumble childhood, there was the worry for the expectant women, the misplaced belief about the psyche of women. The women would not see the killing—a division of labor, a stereotype, and a strange respect.

Dirty work done, we carry the head parts up to the kitchen. I bring Mom's biggest soup pot to the sink.

"Kinda small." Dad says.

"You're kidding." The pot is the largest soup pot I've ever seen.

"You think that's big?" He points to the yard. "That cauldron out there in the front yard, the one that mom grows flowers in? That's from the old farm. That's what we cooked it in."

I had grown up with this pot, had seen it rattling in the workshop, had seen the slow darkening of the metal, then this final rusting relegation to the garden. There are so many pieces of iron and old metal on a farm—pervasive as rocks in the soil, so I had never asked its significance. But now I know: this thing full of petunias was the scalding pot, held heated water that loosened the coarse hairs before you boiled or baked or smoked.

I turn to my father. "So how did you kill the pig?"

He closes his eyes, "There was this pen near the barn where we did it, a fenced-in yard. They tied the pig's snout and one front leg to the post." I watch as the man who is

7

my grandfather raises the huge sledgehammer and brings it down right between the eyes, crushing the skull. Still, it was not the end. Another man steps in, and in the death throes, runs the sharp hunting knife across the pig's throat. And still it is not over. The hobble they have already placed on the back legs is yanked up; they pull the carcass into the air so the creature's blood runs into a clean bucket, or—*if they don't use it for blood sausage*—sometimes onto the earth. They used the blood? I remember that old pig yards are coveted places for gardens. Is it the manure or the blood that makes the soil rich?

"Once the animal was dead, we gutted it. Took out the organs first, set them aside."

"The organs?"

"Oh gosh, those were pickled." He's trying to remember, "How'd they do that?"

Mom picks up, "A heavy salt and vinegar brine. We made it ahead, and the intestines were rinsed to make sausage."

Dad nods. "Then we cut the body. Forelegs, hindquarters, ribs, back, hocks. Some cuts were wired to be hung and aged, some meat was iced. All that."

"And the head?" I ask.

"The last thing, all that's left." But the squeal, I remind them. But even that final voice, the squeal, was used to soften the brutality—a touch of humor to acknowledge they were wasting nothing—if they could have figured out how to use the squeal, they would have.

"Why is it called a cheese if it's really just meat?"

"I think to make it more appetizing. You might not want to eat sliced head." And my mother winks, and they fall into a fit of smirking like kids discovering a bad word. My parents? My parents are so old-school they may have invented old-school; my parents are Catholic and devout, country and self-educated, conservative and strict with themselves and their judgments. But here is silliness, here is an off-color joke between the two of them in the middle of work. This too is survival.

The stories that come from them are not made of storying language, but of utilitarian vocabulary. They are stories that do not guide a life, but guide a living. There is no tradition of aristocracy among these immigrant farmer families, and most fortunes, if there ever were any, have been masked or downplayed by the need not to alert God (or the neighbors) to your success, lest He need to teach you a lesson about being too big for your britches. These are not the Bible stories of high morality, nor fairy tales which shape underlying dreams, nor literary stories of complex character, and not even of our outlaws. These are stories made of how-to, how to get along, get on, build and rebuild, how to use your eyes and ears and teeth to feed yourself and your kids.

My mother studies the pig's head, now in parts, and pokes it with her fingers.

"Yup, that's just what it looked like after it was scalded." She smells it, looking disgusted.

"Is it bad?" I ask.

"Not at all. The skin just smells greasy. We used to love that. You had to have fat to stay alive in those winters—no real insulation, no puffer jackets like you have. That's why pigs were so popular; they had more fat than other animals." She puts her hands on the head, feels around, pressing. "It's fine, but I don't think I want to cook it in the skin. I want to take the skin off and reduce some of the fat. We can't eat like that anymore. We don't work it off like we used to."

My father takes a sharper knife, the fillet knife for fish, and he begins piercing the skin on the brow with a horizontal slit. He will remove it in sections. He and I pull it away from the skull. As it comes loose, the layer of fat is revealed and we scrape some of that. My mother slides the dog's dish our way.

"Here, put the scraps in that." The dog will be delighted. She fingers the ears before she walks away, shakes her head, "Maybe we cooked them with the ears on?"

Dad says, "Not at our house. They were toys." He keeps pulling skin away. Then something happens: the line, *they were toys*, begins to resonate. In that line, narrative buzzes like a fly loose in the kitchen, wandering, wondering, something about small boys under the apple tree, playing in dirt, using an ear to act as a wall in a makeshift bridge with broken bricks, and then the dogs come and steal the ear and the boy kicks the dog and the bitch is pregnant and miscarries what were to have been the prize hunting pups. Then there is the scream, the beating, the lost pups, the lost hours of hunting with a father as dark and punitive as the great mysteries of the church. Did this happen? I see it clearly in my mind. It did not happen. Or not this way. I don't know. This is where story crosses to complete invention, to fictions that rise from imagination's ferment. This is where I stop. If I cross over, I am not listening for connection, old to new, far to near, generation to generation. I am no longer working with the clay their voices offer freely. Then, I am making it up. There is a difference, and I know it in my heart. I stay with the butchering. I stay with head cheese. The ears were toys. That boundary. That image of ears as toys is rich enough.

This is another way the writer, particularly the memoirist, thinks.

My father tears the skin off between the eye holes and the long snout. I help by pulling the loose ends or cutting parallel slits along the sides. When the snout is revealed there is a cracked part of the bone, just below the eye. It doesn't seem to be shattered enough to have knocked a creature unconscious.

"Dad, did they ever shoot them? Wouldn't that have been swifter, kinder?"

"I think they might do something like that now, but we did it the old way. Otherwise, they didn't bleed right. It's still best that the heart is beating while the brain dies. The bleeding is better." The pig's heart beats on for a while as it bleeds out? Inside a body, the beat can go on and on, cyclical and without linear opening and closing? The heart still beating when the brain dies? The mind gone, did the eyes still see? Not the way they do when everything is connected. Death demarcates the place of separation between body and story.

Back in Mom's kitchen, the head goes into the large pot with aromatics: celery and onions and carrots and so much salt I am not sure what is left to taste. Some bay leaf and pepper—she tells me they didn't really use many herbs back then. On the sly, I throw in some oregano.

"How long?" I ask as I set the burner.

"Until tomorrow."

Tomorrow. A whole day to simmer, *sunrise to sunrise* my mother says but it is afternoon the next day, a day when the house scents up with fat and the damp aroma of hearty broth, something like roast, like ham, like anticipation. That afternoon, my father lifts the dripping head from the pot, places it in a large colander where it drains and cools. The drippings go back to the pot. Then that broth too is poured through a sieve to catch the spent vegetables and again returned to the pot. Mom turns the heat on low. It must be reduced, she says, to *about half.* So it jells.

I taste the broth. It is rich; loaded with pork flavors. The bay has collaborated to offer a savory lift that makes a broth and also a spirit.

Still, what is in that colander is a head, the once-upon-a-time thinking part.

Once cooled, we pull off the flesh. It is easy, almost falling away, loosened as loss from the bone. We pile it on the long board, more meat than one can ever imagine in the head. The tongue skin is pulled off and the skin removed. Inside, delicate strands, all of it piling on the board. All that tissue connecting the squeal to the flesh.

My father lifts his sharpest cleaver and rat-a-tats the meat into fine bits. My mother fills three bread tins with the meat, salting and peppering as she goes, and this time, she asks me what herbs I would choose—a nod to my interest. I choose parsley and thyme—she approves. When the broth is reduced, she carefully pours it over the meat, filling the tins, but leaving space for the fat to rise and solidify.

Then into the fridge. It must rest and chill.

The morning I leave, she pulls a loaf, lifts off the fat, flips the loaf. It trembles on the plate, a salty gelatinous brick made of whatever is inside and outside the bone, whatever the animal has given. She cuts the slices. She lays the meat-laden aspic on rye bread and sets it out for my dad and me with mustard on the side. We slather and layer and bite in. I wish I could say I liked it. I do like it, but I also think I need a missing ingredient. I need to be hungrier. That is the trick, isn't it? I need to be less privileged, less judgmental—this is not supposed to taste subtle, nothing fine here. It is instead supposed to fill you up; you were to eat this until the other cuts were brined or cured or dried. And you would live through the hunger.

I need to sink into the hunger that is story. What I have loved most is process. In this case, learning the death of the pig, learning the work to kill a thing in order to live. In this case, hunger feeds the flavor. If you are hungrier, food is more flavorful. I long for stories, to hear them and tell them, long for the flavor of small tales, large tales, tales of the before times. You find the favor in telling, in the longing for them, in the way the longing feeds the living. But you have to be hungry, both teller and listener.

I look at the remains, the bones and gristle that cradle thoughts that an animal has every day of its life, and then it doesn't. I think about the end, when the brain must die but the heart must keep going so that the blood drains—and I know I will write it, write some story of being alive from this death. And something else. As I take living and dying into my hands and my knowing, into my own words, I wonder if I can be a person who hears the squeal, who writes the quotidian voice of the pen. I turn the ear in my hand, filled with gratitude for the pig, the work, the process of making a tale that feeds me.

When Eden Shifts

We were so young, we could barely shape language, but we could run, wildly and with abandon, up the hills behind the farmhouse, through old orchards and then down into the back forty where a wide-fenced pasture with a fresh-running creek made an unfettered playground for four rangy kids. We would risk barbed wire, grumpy cows, and muddy lowlands to arrive at the purity of that stream curving like a sickle through my father's acres. There, in wide sunshine that fell on the narrow creek beds, crayfish, frogs, turtles and small fish grew up just to be captured with makeshift poles and tattered gray nets. With the energy and will of beavers, we constructed small dams of sticks and mud only to see the greater will of the stream wear them down in hours. We stood in the deeper places where the current carved small pools around large stones and cooled our dirty faces and scratched arms in dark apricot water. We sat with our feet in the mint liquid and ate brown-sugar sandwiches and sliced apples from torn paper bags.

Once, while my brothers and I played there, we heard a cow bawling, one of a herd of our temperamental Holsteins. The sound rose from pines to the east which formed a margin between pasture and true swamp, a dark and blurred boundary we had not gained the confidence to haunt. We heard her bawl again more insistently until, as if she were some out-of-key Pied Piper, we began to follow the call.

We scrambled into scrubland, land so poor even the pines looked thin.

In our family, talk was a chittering thread running quickly through the hours but in the sound of pines lived something opposite our noisy souls. Pine words were made of low syllables, nonsentences of slow, dark prayer strung on wind that existed nowhere but there. When we finally entered, our skin cooled, and we turned quiet, stepping silently on the lichen-drift until we found her. She was standing, head low and tongue hanging, and as we watched, her sides heaved.

Tom immediately announced, "She's gonna throw up."

I wasn't so sure. Though I was as protected as a child could be on a farm, I was also old enough that my mind told me things I could not yet express: babies came from somewhere real, from bodies. I remembered my mother's last pregnancy distinctly. I was sure enough to contradict him with sisterly authority. "Nope. She's having a calf."

The cow labored, breathing heavily, and bawled again so loudly that we all stepped back.

"She doesn't look like she's having a good time." This from Rick.

"Is it supposed to hurt like that?" Tom asks. Since I had established myself as the expert and they were pretty certain this territory was exclusive to girls, they turned to me. And though I was growing up on a farm, in the kind of animal openness where eggs hatch in your palms and pups are born in the mudroom, I wasn't sure of specifics. However, the look of this cow seemed alarming enough that bravado abandoned me.

I resorted to honesty. "I don't know."

"Then we better get Dad." My brothers moved as one, small legs churning through the sand.

I stayed as long as I dared. At first, I talked to the cow as I had heard my father talk to riled animals. *Easy, easy does it.* Then, I tried to sing until the cow swung her head toward me with a look so accusing that I have forever wondered if that is why I do not sing. Finally, her distress seemed so clear that there, with pines lowing overhead, I became afraid of seeing her die and left her, running through grasses and wetlands until I met my father and my brothers returning from the barns.

My father took charge, led the way into the pines, and when he saw her, he said, "Got to get her walking." Whether this is professional knowledge or backwoods lore, I've no idea, but he tied her and pulled her until she started moving slowly with him, out of the pines across the pasture until at last she halted at the creek. There, she refused to cross the narrow water, stood her ground despite my father's pulling and pushing, and my brothers yelling until finally—knowing her own time best and accompanied by the rushing creek— we all watched in amazement as she arched and let out a guttural cry until a small black and white bundle hurtled from her backside.

We were startled beyond words. We stared in a light that seemed strange as the art of Easter, illuminated and soft. Then it was gone.

The mama cow turned to the bundle, and her tongue slipped out, and she licked and licked, and my father pulled us away from her so as not to bother her in this essential work. We did not leave, but sat down in the new grasses, and watched for long moments of quiet, moments I could not count; we held the sound of the tongue, the animal's rough textured mouth. After a while, the wet lump began to move, to rise and wobble and take shape. Then my dad, moving in a roundabout softness strange to him, rose to meet it, helped it place its small hooves, trembling, underneath it, and led its snout to the teat. Then, on the part of this wet creature, no small amount of awkward thrusting and headbutting. Once the calf was sucking, once it was in that familiar position flanking the mama, our bodies grew restless with muscle and meaning. We had seen something born. Restless new energy raced through us. We knew a story had been completed.

How to say this: we had felt the force like the creek, and we now knew something new: it doesn't stop, must flow no matter how much one resists or bawls or attempts to change course. We had rested with her in that place where innocence begins its uncharted course through the roughest pastures. In the cow's pain, in the calf's birth, in sitting in the grasses waiting for the new being to be ready to walk, our Eden shifted, merged with both fear and a growing, tenacious curiosity that also may have birthed imagination.

Now we needed to leave the garden.

Coal Nights

Perhaps imagination grows from unlikely unions, from the unexpected confluence of security and fear, or from even more far-fetched combinations—coal and Vicks Vaporub. Or perhaps it is born in a small tent, moist with contradiction.

But first, that farmhouse. In our old farmhouse, a wood-fired furnace held dominion in the cellar, a creature that provided the heat for the uninsulated farmhouse I grew up in. Later, we borrowed money to install a coal stoker—long before the travesties of coal production were acknowledged. There in the cellar darkness, a red metal box the size of a resting pony was loaded with coal, shoveled with black lumpiness from the coal bin, and this contraption "stoked" the furnace with coal periodically, roaring up, pushing the dark lumps into the stoker where it caught and burned. The coal kept the house warmer than it had ever been. Gone were the restless night risings, Dad trundling down the cellar stairs to toss logs onto dying embers. Gone, the coldest nights when the old ducts of the house would deliver only cold drafts through ornate vents laid in the floor of each upper room. Where once the wood heat had faded in the depth of night, and the chill would, somewhere before dawn, invade the uninsulated house and leave us shivering until the wood fire was roused again, now the coal heat would hold, smoldering for a longer time than wood ever could, and offering up warmth enough that the windows would not frost. The house was warm in the mornings, a miracle of the common sort. What my mother realized soon after: in that advancement toward reliable heat, the coal burn created what my mother called "dirty burn," a thin layer of dust sent up through those ducts, an air-borne invisible particulate gathered on surfaces thickly enough that in a few scant days, you could scribble your name, draw stick figures in it. With disgust held tightly in the purse of her lips, my mother would twice weekly launch into a frenzy of dusting, showing us the gray line accumulated on her dustcloth as she wiped down windowsills and counters. It was her personal battle. It was also a health hazard.

Though it would be years before people learned and understood coal's threat, I will say this: I missed the scent of wood burning, the waft of maple or ash or oak—though I could not have told you that. It was as if some quiet but friendly ghost had abandoned us, and in its absence, we were warmer, yes, but a little afraid—the box in the basement sent up its rattling chain song with every stoke. It was not a friendly sound. It did not burn cleanly and that dirty burn may also have been the cause, for those few brief years, of my reoccurring croup. I was a healthy child except for the croup—its name is onomatopoeic. Croup is a disorder of the larynx, a swelling in the throat sometimes caused by irritation, or an allergic response. It is often the precursor to asthma. For me, it was the sudden and repeated onset of a wild animal living in my normally calm lungs.

By then, I was old enough to sleep in a room of my own, upstairs in the old house, the first room to the left at the top of that old stairwell, a single hanging bulb lighting the landing. Mom left the door ajar so that one light cast a column of pale yellow across the faded quilts on my bed. The light was intended to prevent me from being afraid, to offer me a way down the stairs should I have to pee. Later, it was this light I would use to read.

The first time. I woke at night in that bare bulb's narrow path, a strange wheeze in my throat. When I tried to call out to my mother, a dog had come alive, set off an alarm there. No other way to say this—the cough was a bark, a canine *woof* as if a mysterious hound grew inside my chest. By the time I'd managed to find some voice, and had in fact called out, teary and convinced I was dying, the entire house was awake with this cough. And this became the problem. The sound was a hack to wake the dead.

It went away after a day or two, but then a few days later, returned, a whole migration of wild dogs, and every time its nomadic way returned, the whole family—including a toddler who did not always sleep well—awakened to it. There was that rise out of blue float of sleep in that dim room. There was the rough interior alarm in the lungs. There was the in-breath and there again, in the soft dark, it rose, that wild running, loose-dog rattle just under the knobs of my collarbone. I learned to recognize the restless precursor dreams, the sweaty waking, and then the cough would explode, would surface in my throat as an explosive growl.

I don't know how many times I had the croup. I do know that my Aunt Stella, who lived in Muskegon, gave my mother a second-hand vaporizer called a Prak-T-Kal. Aunt Stella said it would do the trick, that the dry air in our house was the problem.

* * *

It is night. The back door of the house slams, signaling that Mom and Dad have returned from a rare night out with church friends. Dad has already left again with Judy, our babysitter from up the road. When Mom takes the first step up the stairs to check on us—her hand on the banister, it is as though she has touched a button. I am there already, sitting at the top of the stairs, trying to hold it in, trying not to cough, but right then my lungs must let go, and then I am wheezing and hacking as though I would vomit. She stops, studies me for just a second, sighs as she always does. She is calculating how long this night will be.

But now she has the vaporizer. She tucks me in to her own bed, fills the glass receptacle with water, plugs it in, and slowly mist rises out of the top. Then she sets it next to her bed, opens the broken umbrella—Grandpa's old black one, and over that drapes the old bath towel, making a gray tent. Then the soft, oh that soft light through the thinned-out parts, and her voice commanding. *Stay under. Don't move. Breathe.* She goes to sleep with one of my siblings. My dad will have the couch.

I am full of hope; so is she. The vaporizer had worked on my brothers and sisters, on their stuffy noses, had resolved any number of congestions. But it was no match; it didn't touch the wolf-dog croup. The coughing does not stop. And then, I know I have disappointed her. Will I ever again be invited to her room, to climb into her bed as I did? The cough remains both inevitable and surprising, like bad days at school, or empty harvests. When she walks so tiredly I can see her stoop in the shadows of the hallway, I pray to not be sick again.

One night I wake in the usual sweat, but this time, it is not a cough but a sharp scent in the air. Not the familiar scent of diapers or laundry or a musty old house. The cough is near but not in me yet. Something else. Something is shifting in that hallway—a floating in the air like a fog, metallic as rusted steel. I climb out from under the old blankets. I wobble down the stairs. I must get to her room before the cough comes on; I must not wake my siblings. When I finally stand by her bed, I touch her shoulder. She turns toward me, "Oh, Anne." Sigh.

"Mom, the house is full of smoke." And then I start. Before I can muster my breath again, she and my father are out of bed, my father racing to the basement, expecting flames, expecting destruction that will be our end. And she hands me a hanky and commands that the boys be woken; she will get the little girls. There is a flurry of rushing, of carrying, grabbing of blankets. We are headed out the back door, headed into the cold when my dad returns, thrusting open every door and window in the house as he moves. *Easy, it's okay now*, he says. The fresh air sets the babies to bawling. The cold clears the smoke. Shivering but breathing, I stop coughing.

The stoker had backed up, the exhaust fan became blocked, and the "dirty burn" became dirtier, sending up the gray plume that sifted through the upper rooms, rising particularly to the hallway with the single bulb. He had loosened the blockage, reset the chains.

The red stoker goes awry twice more that winter. The horse that lives in the basement chokes. Sleep turns even more fragile from the fear that races through the house when my parents, now attuned to its faults, rise and my father pounds down to the cellar and slams open the lid, stirs the coal in the compartment, and sets the chains turning again. My mother opens windows and the cold clears our distempered air. And maybe that's what gave her a clue—because each time, the cold air slowed the cough. She couldn't let the house stay cold, but what would mimic the cold in the lungs?

In between these events of high panic, the wheezing dogs return to me like faithful companions. When she hears the bark rising in the dark this time, she sets up the vaporizer once again. I wonder why she goes to the trouble when she knows it does not help. But this time, she brings something new to the corner of her bedroom, to the small side table, a blue jar with a translucent gray salve that stinks and makes my nose pinch. She fingers a dollop and smears it into the leaky container. She turns it on and lowers the towel. Here, I rest, turned toward the Prak-T-Kal vaporizer. The tiny salve island floats in the water of the glass receptacle, slowly dissolves, and then the air shifts. Cool menthol mists across my face like a soft touch that isn't really a touch, but something like a touch, almost a touch, cool as peppermint but not really mint—stronger, even in that gentility. The word *camphor* is a long way off, but this air is as cool as too-early spring, cool as window glass in frost season. She tucks the shadow tent of my sick world around the old umbrella with the broken tines and for a few hours, I live inside that mist, just the damp brushing against my face, nose, eyes. At first, there is only the longing to not be so alone as I wait for the wolf, the dogs, the pack to rise.

I do not notice the quiet at first. In the dark, in my mother's room, in her very bed, under a pale towel tent, I start to wonder if anywhere in the world, it's different from where I am, if there are places where hallways do not fill with smoke, seen in the wafting light of a single hanging bulb. I feel the drift of my own thoughts—and these odd ideas spiral under the mist of the vaporizer, that small machine that makes water's liquid into mist. And then, just before sleep, I know another true thing: I have not coughed in long minutes. Breath is there, the wheeze eases off, slinks away.

Eucalyptus from another land, from across the world perhaps, a softer creature has entered my mother's warm makeshift tent. This creature is dressed in sheers, dressed in wind. I am alone with the half-sleep that is a dream: a black horse with red markings, a horse nearly but not yet on fire, a smolder rising from its metallic hooves as it strides away, out onto the dark fields of thought. Here is a rumble that will make stories, riding away on the longing, on the dreaming, on the coal smoke of a stoked mind, wolves trailing far behind.

A Map of Hands

Maps, those paper grids spread open on a table, a counter, a bench, all become a narrow way to move through the strangeness of place. They give order to what cannot be seen but that which is sensed in the distance—another place, another space, another source for the three-dimensional. With a map, I become longer-sighted, more architectural. The world, the country, my state become something I can frame, know its contours even when I am not there. Even my home, the farm, becomes more comprehensible. Old paper maps, like language and the grace of a sentence, are one way the world is made tangible.

Maps understand the particular surface of things, and sometimes, they are clues to what is underneath the surface. If you look at a map of the state of Michigan, you will see the proverbial "hand," a wide mitten-shaped peninsula surrounded by and impregnated with water. If you run your finger along the west coast, south to north on the left side of the hand, you may trace two arthritic knots of land halfway between the city of St. Joseph and the Mackinaw Bridge. These extend into Lake Michigan like malformed knuckles. The southernmost one, because of its particular position, because of the westerlies and the warm water currents, is a microclimate and snow belt. Here, though the soil is not nearly as good as the soil in the thumb where farmers grow sugar beets and celery, it still supports a lively agriculture simply because of this climate caused by the land's placement against the lake. The region sports a late spring and a later summer. And though hard frost can still kill spring-blooming orchards, generally speaking, the warm comes late enough so that more years than not, crops that freeze off further north and south manage to survive in Oceana County. It is all any farmer asks for, that the odds will be with them. This is the county of my birth.

On the farm where I grow up, there is first a dairy herd, and when that fails, a beef herd, and when the price falls on the beef market, young as I am, I know our farm is in trouble. I am the oldest of five and I am learning to read this hand-drawn map into which I was born. It is a whole but tattered world. I know things are awry on this map because instead of purchasing new cloth at the yard goods store, my mother remakes church hand-me-downs, something she has never done before in my short life. I know because their voices hold the sound of dry rain as they talk over the old oak table, and because my mother is not happy when my father decides to plant something that is new and unfamiliar, and therefore dangerous.

Asparagus, it is called. What a strange word, a strange sound. Hard to spell. It is a vegetable but sounds like spitting.

I listen. I look at the pictures. With its strange root, skinny green stalk, and far away history—it first grew in a place called Siberia, it seems a poor choice for this family of plain faces chewing noisily over their oatmeal at the breakfast table. And those five acres we stare at through the kitchen window might be used for a quicker cash crop. So my mother claims as she scoops spoonfuls of canned berries onto the cereal, pours whole milk from a glass jar. Asparagus, after all, takes three years to mature. The root stock is pricey. Mom's coffee cup bangs against the kitchen counter. My mother's opinion is the sharp click of that cup. But my father has been reading, a thing he does. He says asparagus is a crop that will come into its own, that more people will eat it, and he has read about California farms with soil similar to the light and sandy soil here in Michigan.

"But they have a longer growing season," my mother argues. "They don't have snow."

"The California farmers make decent money on it." My father speaks and looks straight at my mother. There are more words but that is how this field is decided. Midwinter, with not a penny to spare, he orders the roots for that five acres. I learn the roots are called crowns. Baby crowns. I try to imagine them as circular, sparkling with jewels, like in the fairy tales. But when the burlap bags of stock arrive, they look like tangled spiders.

On a cold April day, the storage barn door is open to let in the thin spring sun. Piles of icy snow dotted with clots of dirt spot the yard like small eruptions. We gather on the cracked cement floor and sit on upside down bushel boxes, and we spend hour after hour carefully separating the matted crowns that have been dug from some place on a map I cannot read, from far south and west of Michigan. We separate the crowns to make them easier to plant. They feel like ghost fingers, spindly wormlike roots radiating from a hard core in the center. That center has tiny knobs sticking up like the beginnings of something—that is the crown. We shake our heads at this oddity.

About those acres behind the big barn, a square of land that had been set to corn, then wheat, and for a while, even potatoes. The borders, if seen from above, would have indicated the smallest quilt square among many large ones, and inside it, the colors change according to the whim of markets I do not yet understand. Still, always in the spring, it is fertilized with manure and then the sweet-sour scent is so strong it drenches the air and makes our noses run. This spring is different: this spring the cut of a single blade plow runs over it, paralleling the surface with furrows deep as the folds in a giant's fan.

On a day laced with sun and bitter north wind, we plant these crowns in the furrows, my siblings and my mother and I, carrying baskets full down each row. My mother moves slowly down the long rows. She is still recovering from mumps, something we had all been sick with that March and every step she takes jars the still sensitive glands in her neck. She tells me she aches all over. We move down the rows, our winter coats dark across our backs, our heads ducked stocking caps, our legs lost in the furrows: we look like large beetles trapped in troughs too deep for us to escape.

It will take many days to plant the field.

My hands turn so cold that I watch from a great distance as my fingers in their thin gloves reach down into the basket for a single crown, lift and drop it, pointy side up, into a furrow. The girl who is me tamps it down with my boot. She glances up into a thin sun, facing the winds, the land, and see the bodies of her brothers and neighbor workers moving slowly over the field. She steps another twelve inches, drops another crown, presses it in, repeats the process step by step down each long row. Every hour or so, an old tractor snorts to life, covers the furrows, buries the work as though these people had not touched every root. It smooths the surface so that no one will ever know how their hands hurt or what hope lurks under this five-acre map.

I am startled back to myself when my mother sighs like a tired wind, and says she can't go on. She goes to the house. We finish without her. It is the loneliest work I have ever done.

That summer, the fernlike plants rise like miniature pine trees, no more than an elbow high, soft fronds spreading like delicate etchings. The next year, they grow tall as a dill plant and are not unlike it. That fall, I watch as these fine green fernheads of the asparagus plant turn from their thick dill green to something I had not expected. After hard frost, when the late October sun falls from the long west across the plants, the tall ferns bend and turn golden as a Bible picture. They are rounded down by weather, and the hounds chase rabbits into the tunnels made by the arching ferns. The dogs flush the rabbits, and my brothers occasionally shoot one for supper. I hear them say in voices that sound as though they need rain that we will have to wait another year before we will harvest this asparagus field. Before we will know. Is it that winter, or the winter after, the beef cattle catch a respiratory illness, and my father has to shoot some of them in the barnyard, and the carcasses are hauled away like bags of dirt? I wear the same winter coat for the third year. But I hold the field as it was in fall; I hold the open and golden space as a map, a square of rippled glowing texture. Here is the rise of sun on the slope, here is the bronze of sunset.

Then there comes a spring when I am taller, when my baby sister no longer wears training pants, when we are all taken to the fields, when finally the stalks rise like spikes from the dirt, come on thick and heavy enough to harvest. This thing, this spear as they call it, is so plain, I am disappointed. It looks like a skinny tree trunk with a curled-up top. It seems impossible to be of worth. But it must be taken, and quickly, before that tip spreads open and it attempts to blossom. We walk down each row, bending and breaking. We toss the stalks into baskets and buckets which we dump clumsily into larger bushels. Though the California magazine claims asparagus should be knife-cut, we break the green stems with our hands, close to the ground. It cuts our knuckles; the juice irritates and dries out the skin. My hands change, thicken to the broadness that will mark my life.

We have picked an entire field. The map is now empty, barren. It was hard, harder than we thought. It took hours, and there was dust in every crease of our bodies; our land, our soil, marking the map of our skin. My mother hauls that first twenty bushels to a processor in our small town, Hart, in the back of our old station wagon. When she returns, she is smiling oddly. There is a slip of paper, a check in her hand, some money. That night, after supper, their voices are soft as they talk.

And then the startling thing. The thing I did not expect. Asparagus comes back, returns, grows up all over again. The plant, once that first stalk is broken off, insists on being, sends another up and out of the earth. It continues to give, to grow, stalk after stalk. Every two or three days more green spears rise, tenacious as growing can be. I come to understand that root crown we had planted years before, the tiny knot of protruding shoots at the center of the spidery roots. The crown. Each tiny protrusion becomes a stalk and the plant is so hardy that it sends dozens and dozens of these shoots up every season, from mid-May to mid-June.

In the face of our tiredness, this plant is tireless.

That first year our family picks the field no more than a dozen times. I earn a quarter a bushel, though I don't think my parents can afford to pay me anything. But it feels like a lot when I count it up. Enough for new shoes, Red Ball Jets if Mom will let me. I know also that something in our household has changed because when at last the season is over, the last picking is announced, and the last slip of paper comes home from the processor, my father and mother take us camping for a weekend—in an old army tent without a floor. That small celebration, almost brazen for a farmer— Dad taking midsummer time to camp, my mother almost relaxing as she roasts hot dogs over a pinelog fire, that is a new map, one we have never seen spread open into our future, showing a way.

Each year, a larger harvest, a longer season as the field matures. The market holds, the price rises. My mother does not complain about the work, though I do—I am discovering that I do not like this work. It makes no difference. The map of work is to be followed exactly. Times are better because of the asparagus field—that early and immediate cash crop, that first vegetable, that sure sell. Small markers, points on a line in a journey. Our hands toughen; our skin always looks rough. We will always have old hands because of this harvest. For the first time, we have enough. My objections are lost.

The next cold April, my father plants more acres and when it comes to maturity, we pick that field too. My mother enrolls me in Catholic School for the first time, as a fifth grader—she confides that tuition comes from the asparagus harvests. Though I am grateful, I am not so much taught by the good sisters as by the requirements of a hard field. As the springs move forward, I learn heat, dirt, and arithmetic in the weight of those green spears, in the number of harvests, in the number of bushels, in the number of beetles that can destroy a harvest—all that multiplication. I learn from the number of scrapes on my knuckles. I learn how, if I hold my right hand out, palm up, it holds a calloused map of work in those fields. That's what this living is, a moving back and forth over the rows, harvesting the green. That's what this is, a picking of green hope, demarcated by bending to a field that both anchors me and from which I must be broken.

Shining Eyes

My father, no saint, indulged in his share of borderline legal activities, including "shining deer." He never poached, but he would venture into cool summer nights, shining a spotlight across the meadows of the Manistee National Forest. *Let's go shining* meant piling into his beat-up pickup and heading to the deep woods, the wide meadows of scrub to find where the deer grazed. While the whitetails stood frozen in light, he counted pairs of shining eyes, commenting on their size, tracking movement, watching for bucks which later in November, he would hunt. He taught us a little of the language of their tails and ears, a bit about tracking. He spoke reverently, quietly, modeling how to be in the wild. But no matter how quiet, on my own, my brothers and I never saw the deer until their white tails plumed away in the distance.

We were bad at this.

We decided we needed practice. With the creative logic of children, we decided to practice on the chickens. We would shine chickens. One summer night we padded down the maple staircase in shorts and jammies, snuck past my mother and father's bedroom, and crept out the kitchen door into the warm summer dark. Skirting the barnyard, we crawled to the chicken coop. There we stopped and argued.

"Let me go first!"

"My turn."

"What if they stop laying?" This would tip off the adults that we had been bothering Mom's prize layers.

"Shut up. You'll set them squawking."

We always set them squawking. With a yellow flashlight and the yelling, we scared the heck out of a couple dozen Rhode Island Reds. If they didn't see us tumbling through the dark, they undoubtedly heard us. After the initial ruckus, they would settle down, clucking quietly, staring dumbly at our light, and we would sit on the edge of a manure-covered roost and talk. We talked about Dad, if he really understood animals, and if our grandfather died because he drank too much, and if we had enough money, and how someday all this practice would pay off. We talked about mom and what she let us do, what we wanted to do, and what we weren't allowed to do. Sometimes, among the chickens and the harmless animal lice, we talked about God. I was the first to ask.

"What's God?"

"Whadaya mean?" Tom sneered. "God's not a what."

"Maybe. Maybe not." I was defensive. It had seemed like a real question.

"Stupid," he'd say.

"Well, what's God like then?" Round and round. God was everything from the benevolent candy man in the sky to the wizard of the woods. We were being raised by devout parents in the strictest of Catholic parishes, but after dark not much of it stuck. My biggest question was why bad things happened. Why had our aunt's baby died hours after it was born?

Once Tom tried to explain, "God's like these chickens."

"God is not stupid." Chickens had become our example of the ultimate stupidity in the world.

"No...," I could feel him groping for words in his own dark. "But you think these chickens are stupid, and you turn on the light and what do you see."

"Their eyes."

"Yea. They're always looking at you. Like they knew you were there all along." I knew he was making it up—his version of a joke. But he said it like it made sense. Through all of this, my other brother, Rick, was always more silent. Except once in a while he'd say, "Yea." He did now. "Yea."

As I grow, as I learn, I walk in the woods almost every day. I'm walking down a hill at dusk. The wind is right. I step through a pine stand and I see three white-tailed winter survivors. I squat, sit still. They browse in the pale light. I shift, look down, the wind changes, and when I look up, I look into their eyes which shine—not with my spotlight but with their own animal light. They watch me with curiosity. They watch me with awareness, with caution, ready to judge. Then the wind shifts. They catch my scent, flash away, and the roar of their silence leaves me lost because for those few seconds, eye to eye, I have rested in a vision much wilder and larger than I am.

Sacred Fear

Place of illusion and nightmare, the underpart of our warm and weathered farmhouse consisted of a Michigan basement. Stone walls. Cracked mortar. Draped cobwebs darkened with soot, typical of its type—a wooden stairway trembling at every step, rocks the size of old boots, a single lightbulb pouring gray-lit pool into the middle of three haunted rooms. The dark coal bin and coal stoker played pawns to a huge stove that stood fiercely in a sand pit, monster of the bowels of our old house. Down there, old hunting and fishing gear hung on the walls like ancient skeletons of lost creatures, tangled ropes and broken tools were stacked like forgotten bones, and always, always, there were the glass jars.

I was afraid of its dark—what child isn't—and of the scent of potato decay and the oily odor of coal, and later, in winter, the rank smell of hounds my father housed there when temperatures plummeted. I was afraid of the stoker, its cantankerous roar, the clicking and shucking of the furnace as the blaze heated in its bowels. Most of all, I was afraid of the silence under that, of everything being muted and excluded from existence.

The place was a landscape of fear where, if I wasn't careful enough, it would erase me. But there, in a cleverly partitioned and shelved alcove, my mother's harvest of canned fruits and vegetables was stored. Because I was oldest, I was often sent to carry up canned jars of peaches, pears, green beans, corn, pickles, beets, and then after our feeding, I was sent back down with the empty jars, rinsed and dry. I could carry four quarts if I was very careful, two in each arm. I was motivated to carry four because then I would make only one trip down. In the summer I was sent again to collect the empty jars, now riddled with winter flies and coal dust, and carry them up again to be filled with my mother's bounty.

I stand at the top of the stairs. The musty draft sweeps up into my face. Below is darkness. There is no switch for the light at the top. The switch is on the bulb below, dangling like a new moon on a thin rope in the middle of the darkest night. With my elbow, I lean toward the wall just enough to touch the damp but not actually lean on it. I use this as my guide. I don't want to touch the wall with its dark strings of web and soot, but my hands are full of glass. Brushing the wall with my forearm is how I keep my bearings down into the dark. Every step I stop, wait for the wooden step to steady. When I reach the bottom, I stop again. I have to do this just right. I have to walk at a diagonal into the dark so that the light chain hanging from the bulb will hit my face or hands or shoulder. I cannot see it. I walk slowly and try to see what cannot be seen. Then the cool chain brushes my cheek and makes my body clench into a small fork of fear. Only once do I miss it and walk into the shallow pit where the furnace rumbles. The jars roll onto the sand.

After that, I always find the string, pull it quickly, and the room lights but only dimly; the dark stone walls are greedy, suck in a portion of light and refuse it return. I begin the short journey across the room to the alcove. With each step, small puffs of dirt rise around my shoes. Only a slice of the light actually falls into the alcove from the larger room.

When I enter, my shadow blocks even that. I force myself to see in the dark, and place the four empty Mason jars in a bushel crate, glass clinking against glass. I turn and in the dark, the shelf where the golden peaches are stacked glows a little with leftover summer. I know there are twenty-seven quarts left, and I reach into the darkness built against the stone wall. I reach out to the sagging shelves, place my fingers on the tin caps, press the top to check the seal—if the seal is broken I will be sent back—pull down two quarts, enough for cobbler, and one jar of blackberries for breakfast cereal. I squint into the dark, check the jar for mold, look straight at the ghosts, say a small prayer, take several breaths, make sure my face is dry, not wet when I step out of that night, back up to the light of family. I turn to walk back, bringing from this place of fear the pale-yellow fruit of sunshine from the cellar of our lives. Promising no one will ever know.

The Secret Place

My brothers, Tom and Rick, build the treehouse in the huge old apple tree behind the farmhouse. It consists simply of a series of boards, warped plywood, twine, and two-by- fours. There is no roof. From there, they reach up, pick, collect, and then throw small, hard green apples down at me, at anyone who passes under except our parents. They catch me sometimes in the garden and whiz the apples. I have a bruise on my arm. It is a new feeling, this being separate from them, this not recognizing them as part of me—until this year, we were three and yet one. After the treehouse, they are separate from me. I like the idea of the treehouse, but I am not allowed in it. I don't like being hit.

On the other side of the house, I look for places to be safe from the crab apples. I find the grape arbor. A twenty-foot rectangularly-framed contraption, laden with old Concord grape vines. At one end of the arbor, an old cedar grows, and the vines climb up the cedar, wrapping around the stringy bark, and under that, an entry of sorts, so that on my hands and knees, I can squirm into a dappled darkness unlike any other. In the confusing, noisy, often irritable world of the farm, a quiet hollowness. I understand that I need its spotted shade, need the grape leaves larger than my father's hands, the tangled vines, more than I need a treehouse. I climb into the cool interior space framed by the ancient hemlock posts and crosspieces that sag but hold. Those gray logs lace themselves vines, weighed down with grapes that hold a thousand green worlds. Unmowed weeds launch an insurrection around the edge of the arbor, forming a thick boundary, but under the vines, dry clay. No sun calls up the weeds and so the floor is clear, a small dirt chamber walled by vines. There among harmless spiders and small summer flies, I peek out at the backyard to watch my mother hang laundry on the lines, the stained squares of towels or diapers marking the years, or see my grandmother hobble to the garden for beans, my brothers shouting in the barnyard, my sister climbing into the rabbit hutch.

What June of what year is it that I began to say no to that world?

When the grapes are still tiny spheres and the leaves still a large green patchwork tenting summer's brittle light, I hear their call and refuse it for the first time. Was it after peeling peaches for hours, or after hoeing the corn seedlings, or perhaps not after any of those things, just after a quiet morning when I want more of this hollow space, this cave of my own strange light?

This inside thing is like my other inside things; it is happening in my mind.

This is a greed which I do not resist.

Again and again, my mother's voice, then my grandmother's, then others rise over the yards and fields, calling my name. I realize that they are not worried yet, that they want me to work, and that they cannot find me to do that work. I know I should leave the dark and go pull my sister out of the rabbit hutch before she gets lice, or I should help hang laundry or cut beans. But I stay and listen to where they are, to the subtle change in register. Or stare into the delicious coolness until I enter the reverie of a young girl finding her first privacy in a household so wildly chaotic and lively that privacy is foreign gold.

I refuse to answer them.

Of course, my mother catches me. Whether she sees me enter the arbor or simply hears me talking softly to myself, she is angrily efficient about yanking aside the vines and crawling into the hollow space on her hands and knees. We face each other silently, she is red-faced and sputtering, me pale and sullen with the knowledge that I have pushed too far from needs that organize a large family on a working farm. She scolds me sharply but when it is done, and she stops for breath, she holds silence for a moment, her gray-brown hair falling into her face. She looks at me. I can't meet her eyes because I am so ashamed. But she sees some other thing in the torn tee shirt, the curl of shoulder. Or remembers something.

She sits back on her heels, bits of draped vines catching in her hair, "You come here a lot, don't you?"

I nod. She waits; something she does not do easily. Haltingly, I tell her. About watching, thinking, talking to myself. She listens with her face turned away from me a little, staring at the still green grapes, shadows falling across her face. She sighs, nods. She says quietly, "You have work to do. You'd better get to it. You're the oldest; you know that."

Know what? That being oldest means being more obedient, harder-working, more *with her?* But before she backs clumsily out from under the vines, she looks at me with sadness I have never seen, and says, "You can come here after supper. I won't tell the boys."

I rarely come after that, knowing on some deeper level that despite my mother's grudging permission, rebellion is not a force an oldest girl can rightfully claim. Only once in a while, when the farmhouse which for all its love, is too unsafely communal, and I need the singularity of a secret place. And in those rare dusks, as the night sounds begin to rise and the mosquitoes whine in the heat, I figure out what it is I need. It is not so much refusing after all, but that I can be more myself without them. I can be separate in a way the boys are separate in the treehouse, except without the need to throw the green apples. Or maybe it is a way to throw apples, this being alone. And there is something else. I can be empty too, for a while, like space itself. My hands do not need to hold theirs, or anything. But even more, nothing in me *needs* at all for a while. That will change later, but not right then.

I will not have words for this for years: but it is hollowness that will shape my breath. And when I come away from the arbor, the world will still be there, and I will enter it, say *Yes, I'm here* again and no one will know about this dangerous emptiness that is flying through the air to strike me so quietly and so hard I am black and blue with understanding.

Tears

In the front yard of the farmhouse grows a silver maple with a canopy the size of a green cloud. Over the roof of the house it hovers, old and loud. Its silver leaves are stiffer than other maples, so its voice is of a higher tone than the sugar maple cousins. The leaves, tinted on top with night green, have an underside that steals light from the stars, and when they turn in wind, the entire tree shines like green foil. Under those branches, I shoot up, a brown weed in the shade. Under the tree, I shape my first stories.

What grows in me is lawless thought, or at least lawless compared to my steadier, more stoic brothers and sisters. Under the leaves, I grapple with the things I understand least. Of all of those, the one I am most flummoxed by is Death. I try to get to its meaning, it's strange power over my old aunts and uncles, even the grass, even the air—for my father has said there is dead air in the silo. I have been to my first funeral. My Uncle John died when I was five. At his funeral, he was in a coffin, a metal bed made up with shiny sheets like I had never seen before. They tell me he has gone to heaven and is never coming back.

Why not? I ask.

You can't come back from heaven.

Why not?

Because, they sigh finally in exasperation, *you are dead.*

I go to six funerals before I am twelve, two of them babies.

In the stories I am making up, I practice death. I try to create its drama, its amazement. I try to reckon with what I already know is its inevitability. One way I do it is to invent a monster who kills me, who comes and cuts my head off, or pierces my heart with a fang. I am killed time and time again. I lie in the grass in the position of the bodies in the coffins. Or I die of illnesses whose names I have learned from my elders, but for which I have no real understanding. What does the word diabetes mean to a girl? Or heart failure? What is heart failure? I hide in the chicken coop, the barn, under the mock orange bush and act it out. I can be destroyed by the evil spell of liver cancer from a witch, or trapped in vines of hardening arteries which squeeze to death. I stagger, dying. I run, dying, I crawl, dying, to the front yard, to the silver tree.

And every time I come back to life. A thousand times. Under the maple, life is never over. It never ends. The worst nightmare of death is erased in the tree's shadow and life is always called forth by the simple turning of leaves to their silver side.

That tree is a constant wonder even before I know what wonder is.

* * *

One spring, after the long winter during which I had lost my grandfather to something called a stroke, my grandmother comes to live with us. She sits near the dining room window and looks out and cries. At first, I try, along with my little sister, Marijo, to sit with her, but after a few times, her grief seems so endless that I become afraid. Though my sturdy sister stays with her, I can't go to Grandma anymore, not understanding a mourning that can be longer than winter.

I can't figure out what it must be like for her to love my grandfather so much she cries for an entire season. I miss him perfunctorily, his cigarettes and his jokes and his card playing and his quiet. But I can't know what bond would have to exist for her to cry at the window all those months until April.

Instead, I play outside the window, under the tree with its golden-brown buds and its tiny yellow leaves. Sometimes I look toward the house, stare at her through the dining room window, outside to inside, and see her with her face turned from the interior of the house, from the family, turned toward the outside but not seeing me. Never seeing me.

But I can watch her even through the glass. Her white curls surround a face distorted with sorrow and the shadows of maple branches. Even so, I forget. I lose myself in story. I stand under the tree, act out my own destruction at the sword tip of an evil knight or the poison of a red apple. I lie in the muddy grasses, dead, and then, with flare and aplomb, rise from the dead.

She never notices. She is staring into a dark I cannot see yet, cannot comprehend.

One day, my father trims the maple. The long branches bang against the porch roof and grow so low they brush the ground. My mother wants something that looks more tamed. She has planted peonies and lily of the valley, chosen outdoor chairs and a table. She is trying to bring order to the rangy yard. The tree must be trimmed back so there is a place to set these things—to make a picture of a lawn like you see in Home & Garden magazine. I watch as my father takes the pruning loppers to the low skinny branches. His arms reach up, lengthened by the tool, and he opens and closes them like a bird's beak, snipping the low branches, letting them fall onto the matted grass. He uses the chainsaw on the larger limbs. The whine cuts through the winds of early spring, and then we help him pile the branches onto a flatbed and he hauls them to the burn pile.

When he is done, I walk back under the tree, under newly opened spaces. There are empty places now for the sun, but they fill me with sadness—was that open space where the stories were kept? I want the spaces filled in again, tangled as mystery, filled with imagining; there is too much light here. I walk in circles under the tree. Where are the places that resurrected me? Why is the voice of the tree quieter now? I turn to the window. There is my grandmother, as she always is, at the window, looking out.

She is not crying.

Today she is watching the tree.

Why, after all this time, is her face dry?

And then, on my arms, in my hair, I feel what she is seeing. The sap drips from the wounded branches. All over the yard, wherever the branches were cut, a slow rain falls, and it is this, maple tears caught in the low afternoon sun, golden singular shards of sweet water, that have shifted her vigil at the window. And as I stand watching her, sap dripping on me, I begin to suspect something of how grief might work, that there might come a time when something irreplaceable could be taken and could never again be brought to life, and only if the light is right, if another version of tears is offered, could one find a way to dry one's face.

Smudge

Weather obsesses farmers. The cycle of frost and thaw are so important that some farmers will not say hello before they ask, "How cold wazzit your place last night?" My father is a man who shows friendliness by explaining the weather to you. "See that cloud line? Cold front coming." If my father talks with me about weather's effect on crops, he is saying he loves me. If he does this with men or friends, he is showing respect.

It is a Friday night in May, and I am a sophomore in high school and my friends are coming that evening to play guitar and sing songs in our half-remodeled garage. I help my mother dust barnwood sills, shake braided rugs that cover the concrete floor of the garage. As I clean, I fantasize about taking a late walk with Nick, the boy I like, through our blooming moonlit orchard, thinking how romantic. Romantic, with the trappings from roses to candlelight, is something I want.

Then on the 6:00 local news, hard frost warnings. Even then, I don't think about the weather except to wonder if it will be too cold to kiss under the trees. I miss my father watching the thermometer all evening. I miss my mother pacing the kitchen, looking out at the orchard where my dad drives the pickup through the orchard rows. I am too absorbed in preparing for the garage party, my first, to see him walk out among the trees and will away the cold. I am having friends to my house. I am thinking about kisses.

They arrive. It is the sixties but we live in a community so rural that it will be two years before bell-bottom jeans and big collars hit our world. We talk about "hippies" as though they are aliens, but we're all curious. The summer of love hasn't been conceived of yet. The Vietnam war is a vague threat too far away to worry about—though before we graduate college, two of the four boys in that room will be drafted. We make pizza from a box. I pick out the chords to "Blowin' in the Wind" on the guitar. We stack Beatles' forty-fives onto the spindle, push aside the second-hand chairs and dance to "Help, I need somebody…" The cold is something we slip into only to dry our sweat before the next song drops.

At eleven o'clock, my father's dark shadow enters the house. I am barely aware of my parents in the kitchen, talking in a tone which, if I had been listening, I would have recognized as desperation laced with cold. But when my father comes into this unfinished room where our bodies are wild with motion, his face is dark. He smells of diesel, and I know. So do most in the room—we are, despite our reputations, alert to adults, tuned to their moods. We know when something is off.

He stands quiet. Someone turns off the music. We still our restless bodies, looking at him. We expect to be scolded; we have been too loud. There will be no chance for kisses.

He looks at Cliff, at Nick, at all of us, a mix of ragtag kids who have grown up in rural life so thick with weather trouble that we can sense it the way city kids can foretell rush hours and unsafe streets. It is there in my father's breathing. His words vary the song, "I need some help here, somebody to…" And he explains.

He hands the boys work gloves, and my mother passes out old sweaters so school jackets won't get filthy. I hurriedly pull on jeans and sweatshirt, and we find old pants for the girl friends. My mother calls parents to inform them of this peculiar draft. Everyone understands; everyone knows this story.

Out in that shadowed world of frail blossoms and cutting chill, we follow the pickup through the orchard trees. My father shoves bales of heavy hay off the tailgate, and behind him, the boys lift and place them between trees, and carefully light each bale, one or two under every few trees. Too compact and green to burn, the bales smolder and hiss, but do not erupt, and that warm smoke rises, carrying with it the few degrees that may, if we are very lucky, prevent the blossoms freezing.

As I bend to each bale, I wonder why he doesn't use smudge pots, then remember his complaints about the price of oil. He doesn't have to pay for the hay, it's his, though he might have to buy more come fall. As the night grows colder, and we move through the dark laced with headlights and flashlights, I listen to my siblings and friends move steadily among the grasses. "Blowin' in the Wind" runs in my head, and I know, if the wind would come up, the warmth would circulate, but it is still as a stone under those trees. I sing crazily, "How many rows must a man walk down…" No one laughs. The moon rises so brightly it douses the stars of this bitterly beautiful night on which I had hoped to kiss. We all walk and bend and lift and heave the bales into place. There is only hard breathing, the groan of the pickup on the slopes, the thunk of bales hitting the dirt, the dull lisp of torches—the hard chords of work permeating the ephemeral and silent beauty of cherry blossoms, their sweet scent mixing with acrid smoke and the ghosts of last fall's alfalfa and clover. The new smoke rises, hangs in the dark, a frayed cloud.

We reach the high east hilltop of the orchard land well after midnight, a place where the trees are not planted—too open to weather. The moon finally pours down shrill light. From this high spot, here and there, we can see the dull orange of low flame where a bale or two have ignited, but are burning slowly. But mostly, the smoke spreads like snakes above and among the orchard trees, coils in dark wreaths. The orchard has become an island clotted with a gray snake, floating on black grass. My father, looking west in the moonlight, points to a line of darker darkness shown only because there are no stars there. "Front moving in," he says softly. I feel his relief; a change in the weather. Clouds will capture warmth, raise the temperature. He looks down at the orchard, "Should be enough." He won't know for a day or so, when the dirty blossoms will show themselves saved or not.

He looks at my friends, at their dirty faces. In the silver dark, he takes off his gloves, nods into their smeared eyes, shakes their hands. "Go to the house," he says. "There will be coffee."

We all walk down into the orchard, barely able to see through the haze, quiet with our work and wonder. Nick takes my dirty hand in his. We walk slowly all the way. We do not talk. We do not kiss. The blossoms darken with smudge and future.

The Unwatch

We are still young, but we have not yet lost each other. This is long after we knew Santa was a myth, but before we knew ourselves deeply enough to see our differences. By then, that time when we were in our late teens and early twenties, we knew that Santa was the first great cultural lie for children to grapple with, a sanctioned if difficult way to separate reality from story, the way we learned that fairy tales and Easter bunnies were unreal, the way we knew that adults could play with truth. We already saw the necessary evil of all that. We were not young, but did not know yet the whole truth. Adult yes, but still young and ignorant of what time does. There is sometimes a moment on the cusp.

As small children, my four siblings and I had made a tradition of watching for Santa on Christmas Eve. Five restless kids in frayed pajamas waited at the single-paned, north window of the old farmhouse, poking ribs, fighting for space at the glass. We breathed away thick frost on windows so old they no longer held caulk, and through those frost holes, we could stare, watch for Santa's sleigh to slide under the yard light that splayed its blue cone of light on the snow. We placed our hands on the glass and melted handprints on the window until we were scolded. We tumbled against each other like puppies, too young to think through the absurdities of the myth we believed would arrive any minute.

51

By the time of the unwatch some of us had already suffered. Still, the unwatch remained a time of relative innocence, a time when we could all still come home, when we could come together in a coveted camaraderie. None of us were married yet, and even if we had steadies, they were welcome at the farmhouse at Christmas.

With our somewhat surprising entry into adulthood, the childhood "watches" had faded, replaced instead by "unwatches." Now, we are too cool and too old to admit that we still delight in "watching," a process that takes us back to another time when we did not yet feel the underpinnings of transition. Over time, we develop its opposite, the "unwatch." These unwatches evolve just as our parents decide to clean out our rooms, spilling the posters of rock bands whose names we have forgotten into the woodstove. This is another sign, but we are not yet watching closely enough.

Yes, Mom has told us to take our stuff. She's packed that stuff into tidy boxes we don't have room for, so we do what most kids do, especially at the holidays. We come home from college, step into her warm kitchen, and the old scent of farmhouse wraps us into a blanket of homing. We drive the blue highways skirting our Michigan orchards to the old white farmhouse where for years our parents, having pretty good survival skills by then, sponsor the *unwatch*. We come home. Not to watch, but to make a game, a charm, a tease, of not watching. How many years did it last, this cusp between homecoming and taking the boxes. Five? One?

There were rules.

Rule One: We have to arrive home in time to drink hot cider laced with brown liquor. We have to drink just enough of this to be loose and laughing but not enough that our mother scolds us for being too silly to attend mass.

Rule Two: We attend midnight mass together, crowded into two long pews where we are only occasionally reverent. We sing our own version of carols, reinventing verses that would have shocked the choir if they could have heard the words we mutter just loudly enough for those in close proximity to hear. "Oh, little ton of battered ham…" was typical of these fractures. We occasionally get the giggles so badly that we'd receive the stink eye from the priest. But mass is merely the rite of passage that leads to the Unwatch Breakfast which occurs, not in the morning, but in the middle of the night, beginning after we drive the miles back to the farmhouse, back to that battered nest.

Rule Three: We are not, wouldn't be caught dead, watching for Santa. Santa is a mercenary figure invented by nineteenth-century card companies to turn a quick profit, didn't we all know? Santa is the propagation of commercial enterprises that take advantage of small children and old people. We are above all that. While we were NOT watching for him to show up, we try to catch each other watching. This behavior produces conversations that border on the ridiculous.

"Hey, Dad, how come you're up this late?" I ask

"I'm keeping company with your mother." He winks.

"I think you're watching for Santa."

"No, I'm flirting with your mother."

"You're sure you're not waiting for Santa?"

"Look at this woman. Do I need to think about Santa?"

This was before anyone had lost their heart to a breakup so bad it forced us to take medication, before anyone had lost a marriage or miscarried.

My brother Tom asks my sister, "Hey Marijo. Why you staring out the window? Watching for Santa?"

"Just looking at the stars." Very coolly she says this. She's too cool to hassle.

"You're looking for the reindeer, aren't you?"

"I'm looking at the Big Dipper."

"Star light, star bright, where's that star stud tonight?"

A chorus of groans. Within a couple of years, she will give up a child for adoption.

"Hey, you're singing Christmas carols." Rick accuses Patti.

"I like them." Patti's humming.

"You're trying to lure Santa."

"With this voice?"

"You got that sinus infection again?"

"Thanks soooo much."

This was before anyone had hurt anyone else.

Rule Four: We had to promise to take all the stuff. But we never do. If we leave it another year, we will have to come back.

Though we had always bickered, and sometimes argued, this was before language among us became dangerous, before what is said becomes not unforgivable, but so distancing we could not find each other again. We have no idea that the teasing we do about not watching for that gregarious jollydom in a red suit is the last vestige of family unity. We are not watching for the myth of generosity that flies in a sleigh pulled by reindeer. We are not watching for a myth that ended a couple of decades before. We are remembering, but not watching, not looking back.

We are on the cusp of losing what we do not know we have. We don't know what's coming; families never do. It is time for loving others more. We can't yet say it; we know it, but it is unspoken. We are unwatching.

We sit around the oak table, eating homemade venison sausage and scrambled eggs with green pepper and Velveeta. We talk until dawn, covering everything from the price of cherries to the price of a wedding dress, from making mulled wine to making babies. We make another pot of coffee and pour eggnog laced with the last of Dad's cheap whiskey. We linger and yawn and pretend not to wait. Through this long unwatch, we have been together. We have not crossed over into the complexity that will mark a true adulthood. We believe in ourselves and this family. This unwatch, this not watching for a myth to return because it has not yet left us, is the last gesture of togetherness.

We stumble away from the table at last, and find places to rest for a few hours. We do not exchange gifts until morning, do not yet open the poorly wrapped presents, do not yet belong among those who left the farm. The future is not in the watching, but in pretending not to. Instead, we had come again to the single-paned window, breathed away the frost, looked through the glass into our own small darknesses, poked each other in the ribs and placed our hands on the cold plate of the unknowable future. Sometimes we see stars, but mostly we find our own and each other's breath, the one miracle we never grow out of, that we need only the smallest of guises to reenact as something it is not.

When did we stop believing in he who brings gifts? Everyone remembers that moment when you realized the lie and then also, the next stage, when you participated in breaking it to someone else, or you carried on the lie. It is that transition: the betrayal that must be avenged, the betrayal that must be continued. That's the complication of the unwatch. For us, the unwatch held a contradiction that kept truth at bay for longer than in most families, and for a while protected us, that pretense, even as we knew exactly the irony. Maybe it was a form of denial; maybe we were late in growing up. And then we did. But to a one, we all remember the place where the glass warmed with a hand print, before it was broken.

Part II

The Heart of Place

Every day is a journey, and the journey itself is home.

—Matsuo Bashō

There are a thousand ways to kneel and kiss the ground; there are a thousand ways to go home again.

—Rumi

The Heron and the Pigeon

"It shakes up your bones," I insisted with immense superiority as I stacked boxes on the porch of the farmhouse where I grew up, where I had lived my formative life. I said it as if shaking up your bones were the best thing that could happen. As if my mother didn't know the dark side of being shaken up—usually by me. I was moving out of the farmhouse in order to move in to some unknown, clearly ramshackle, probably roach-infested apartment on a college campus. "Keeps you from collecting too much stuff," I called over my shoulder. She looked skeptical, knowing things I didn't.

I couldn't wait to leave.

During the long phase of educating myself, when I moved a couple dozen times in ten years, I could get the bulk of my possessions into a beat-up hatchback. I embraced moving with a relish that only the young and immortal can maintain. If it hurt me, I forgot. If I lost things, I would borrow. If I had to say good-bye to friends, I would make new ones. I hit the road, accelerated the old hatchback to its maximum sixty-three miles per hour, and enjoyed the tree-fence-fields racing by as I headed for the city or school or any new place to drop my stuff and sleep. Everything, even urban sprawl, seemed new and exciting. I wanted that sunny rush of discovery, of the fast nest or no nest at all. I was not bothered by the kaleidoscope of impermanence. I was, despite being raised up in deeply rooted farm life, a natural traveler, a nomadic creature with an irregular migration. If metaphor helps, a totemic identification, a heron then, in more ways than one.

The heron is a wanderer, often breeding on its northern edge of a huge territory, then flying to different places in other parts of its territory, but not predictably. Its young are ready to fly in a bare two months—striking for such a large bird. Imagine that first flight for such a tall bird— like finding out who you are. And then that amorphous, far-flung internal map—nothing set in stone for this bird. Even when they hunted, their stillness, their sudden strike, and then, having disturbed the peace of the shallows, their decision-making flight—legs trailing like lines to a poem. Off to another shore. Where the fish are. Their wandering, their way of living on many shorelines, I identified with it all.

It's never that simple, that idea of one way of Being. There's also homing, a need for the familiar, for the nest. I am also that, the plump and silly pigeon, the dove who races back, huddles in the familiar barn. At different times, I have headed right for what the pigeon professionals call a loft, the roosting site these birds are instinctively drawn back to, to which they will home—homing, a verb in this case.

During my college years, that *loft* was the family farm-house, that sprawling white-clapboarded, screen-doored, wide-windowed, worn-out structure on a slow rise in a rural township of Oceana County. During those schooling years, I returned most Junes but never for long. By the end of August, I was ready to leap out of my skin, back into flight. After years of wandering school to school, I graduated, and though I made a real effort, I discovered I couldn't stay home, couldn't even rest there for more than a couple of weeks, and after a while, not at all. One reason was that my mother and I no longer found each other good company. And the other? I needed my own loft.

I didn't know that yet.

Missing the irony entirely, I finally rented a small red farmhouse near Grand Rapids and with a gang of like-minded, hippie friends—a small flock of my own— reclaimed it from abandonment. There was an orange stain in the bathtub where the alcoholic owner had once brewed beer. There, the well went dry in July, and we bathed in the spring-fed gravel pits until the drillers restored the water—draining our small budgets. The basement flooded in a series of storms that set down a tornado not a mile from the place, but by golly we protected the one marijuana plant that grew in the garden alongside the tomatoes. One evening, as I ran down a frisbee across an unmowed lawn with a wild-hearted hound at my heels, I wondered what it would be like to stay, to play here, to sit on the porch for a while and to watch the lightning bugs in the fern meadow for, well, not forever, but for a long time.

It could not last. Of course, after we harvested the weed, we all fell apart. The heron is a wanderer. By fall, I was in grad school again, in another apartment, and though I looked longingly back over my shoulder at the red farmhouse, I figured I was done with homing, done with that longing—I mean *what was that?* Off again, yes, but in between, there was a bluff with the long view to the horizon, somewhere... *anywhere* else. From caves in Colorado to delivering a car to Florida, life was turning into one long, exploratory flight. That restlessness.

But not quite. Again, in my final months of a grad program, I stared out my apartment window and saw a woman planting bulbs in a yard across the street. She had one of those special tools that makes the hole just the right size for the bulb. I wanted one of those tools that hollows a place in the dirt. I wanted some bulbs of my own. I remembered my mother planting bulbs that would come up year after year, and she would—there is no other way to say this—smile at them. I recalled her pride in her perennials; she could expect a certain thing to grow in a certain way year after year. Certainty. It made her happy. I had defined myself in contrast to her. I didn't know defiance is a short-lived satisfaction.

That was also the year a friend, Kathy, was killed in a car accident, and the boy I played guitar with at church was diagnosed with leukemia and died before I could say good-bye. Then, the last grandpa passed. Standing at my far-citied window, a Batik print curtain thumb tacked to the frame, I felt tired. In any of the moving pictures in my head, I had not seen these griefs coming, these moments of loss and of longing for a finding—not the white farmhouse, not the red one, but to be in a place long enough that something I had planted grew and bloomed. Stayed alive. It occurred to me I would like to put up curtains that didn't have to be tacked because they might actually hang for a full year. A homing.

It should not have surprised me. It should surprise no one. A sense of place runs strongly through my entire family and through our species. And perhaps having been born on a farm creates a more powerful, if latent, rootedness in rural folks. Tulips can awaken it. Even during my most heron-like years, when I strayed overseas to cities where whole nations of adventures lived, my father's two-hundred acres in West Michigan was the gnomon. Those rolling hills and tree-filled terrains, wide fields and ramshackle buildings became rough model for a place of my own. I didn't want that particular place, not that farmhouse, but I wanted to feel about some place as I had that white clapboard. I wanted to feel the homing, the return to the loft, the arrival.

With job in hand and degrees behind me, a first husband holding my hand, where I arrived was an ordinary tract house in a row of tract houses on a gravel road, a starter home so small and conventional it was textbook, a rectangular box with two bedrooms—the siding a clear sky of blue, a place as simple and unassuming as the nest of a barnyard pigeon. But a kitchen, tiny deck, a backyard unmowed and complete with free-wheeling weeds. A frisbee and a dog. No marijuana plants this time. I hung curtains from second-hand dowels, painted the living room mauve and peach, nailed up family pictures, and built bookshelves. I allowed myself to love that small blue house so deeply that one letter to my parents from those early years reads, "I think I have finally found my place and can cut the apron strings." I was not yet awake to the fragility of home or marriage; how hard it would be to contain both contentment and fidelity. I was as the pigeon is—blindly following the electromagnetic waves of the sun to a roost, to tuck my head under a wing, cling to security that was not fitting a wanderer.

Now, if I travelled at all (conferences, country holidays) I had an itinerary with a date of return. Somedays I never looked any further than my striped wallpaper for contentment. It seemed idyllic, didn't it? It seemed there was some quiet light at last.

Except for that husband, the one who was a musician, who wrote sweet songs and turned heads, the one I loved for the dreams he gave me. To put it directly, turns out he was playing around—in more ways than one. Not just bars but other beds. It sounds like a country song, and he would sing it beautifully and without a trace of irony. The last verse was our divorce—he was leaving me for someone else. Betrayal, among humans and even among birds that mate for life, is common.

He left. I stayed in the house.

Tight as the money was, I had the means. Just barely. I clung to "homing" as the armor against loneliness I had never before experienced. By then I had braided rugs and futons and plates that matched. By then, I barely remembered the days when I lived as a heron, when I was a master packer, when I loaded an entire household, including a bike, into that proverbial hatchback. Now, the bike had been twisted when the woodpile fell on it, so it never handled as well. The hatchback was now a used sedan. I had planted bulbs; the curtains had hung until they faded. It might have ended there. I might have stayed.

I am speaking in narrative summary—mine is about to become a story so familiar, so clichéd as to need only summary and not scenes. Still, still, there was that moment when the heron looked at her monotony, and considered the direction of her life.

Not to anthropomorphize.

But yes, there came this man, of course, at a storytelling circle, people gathered around a bonfire to recite poems, tell tales. I saw him on the edge of firelight, listening. Someone was playing a cello, someone knew the entire "Casey at the Bat" poem, someone yelled the umpire's line, *Strike one, strike two*. With authority. I looked around; it was he. Sometimes, I am not a bird of any sort. I am a woman.

Or a fish swimming toward a small chunk of bread.

The heron has this great trick. If you try to feed it a small chunk of bread, it will accept it, but will not eat it. Instead, it will carry the bread to a place where it knows fish live, and will drop the bread right in front of where the fish are, stand very still and wait. It baits the fish. When the fish swims toward the bread (or the insect or the worm), the heron will nab the fish. I am lured by the bread, this man. I am baited by my own kind. His name is David. The name means beloved.

David lives in Chicago. I live in northern Michigan. Once we decide to see each other, we meet in the middle, in random cities halfway between Traverse City and Chicago, in what I call clandestine trysts—though we are both adults and single, so I'm not sure what is clandestine—though the trysts, yeah, trysts they are. We never know quite where we will stay, or eat, dance, drink—nothing for sure except the great sex. Grand Rapids becomes a favorite midway—that totally Middle American city with its phallic Amway Grand tower, gentrified town center, a hundred churches—mostly deeply conservative Christian Reform. It gives us fits of sardonic laughter. *We're doing this here?* We feel anonymous and at the same time, renegade, like we are pulling off some spiritual heist in that city of Biblical culture. We are role-playing invaders. Secret adventurers. It is illusion of course, but fun, and life hadn't been fun for a while.

After each tryst, I drive home, back to the blue house, to the place where I have planted trees that are now taller than I am. There, tulip bulbs grow prolifically. I am beginning to understand that a choice is coming—that there is a change in the electromagnetic fields. On a practical level, more than ever, I dread how hard it will be to move. What to do with all the stuff that has been part of loving the blue house. I have a matching set of everything from Mr. Coffee makers to cats. A house is a loft is a nest is a place with stuff, including tulips.

But I like the trysts, the eager sunshine of packing the car for a long and stolen weekend—the rushing miles, the coming together in a strange room, near strange waters. The dancing and the way we surprise each other. Can't I have both? The loft and migration?

Eventually the bait becomes even more alluring. David learns what I love: takes me to museums, to galleries, to the theater. He can talk sports *and* art. We dance in an urban atrium nine stories high on Valentine's day. I buy him baseball tickets. He buys me broad-brimmed hats reminiscent of Audrey Hepburn's. We are creating a mating dance that people watch with envy, so perfect it should have been a rom-com, a movie; we pretend it is. I find it titillating, and also, because David is all in, bonding. He too is a heron, albeit a wiser one than I am, and this is a courtship ritual laced with brown liquor, sushi, and trips to the racetrack. Who knew betting on racehorses could be a turn on? With great humility and with much surprise we discover each morning we are together that we cannot carry out the "long-distance migrations" we thought so perfect in the evening. For the first time I am not thinking of how I will go "home" to Williamsburg, but how I will live with this man, wherever he is. I am following the bread.

Vulnerability

For a long time after the divorce from the first husband, I kept that blue house, complete with porch that leaned, garage that flooded, and even though I went away, I always came back. I had been asked if I could move, if I would bear city living, and I just didn't know.

Homing pigeons lose their way. Instead of the myth that they always come back to the loft, the truth is that they may be disoriented by sunspots—the electromagnetic energy of the earth gone awry, by sonic disturbances, by cellphone towers. Sometimes they are just plain lost. In the professional homing races, as many as half may not return.

I could always find my way home. I was learning how to take care of the nest alone. Woodstove, roof, yard, snow, bills. Some days I felt downright badass. I was managing the tough stuff by myself. And with David as my long-distance lover, we were doing fine as weekend nomads, weren't we?

But then, there was this moment.

There exist challenges when one lives rural life to the fullest, and the blue house was not invulnerable. Things went wrong. From smoking woodstoves to corroded faucets, from trouble with your neighbors' target practicing to worms in your favorite trees, few places offer the head-on collisions with the ordinary breakdowns like living rural. But still, I was resourceful, I was capable, I could do it. I could manage it all.

I just didn't expect the raccoons.

What harm could these curious, bumbling, nearsighted creatures do? That's how I perceived them before they revealed their true natures. Maybe they are like that, but the raccoons of Deal Road turned out to be a different breed, kin to Mad Max road warriors or Orson Welles' aliens.

By then, I was teaching adjunct college classes, attending workshops, directing theater in Traverse City. In between trysts and my cliched escapes into romance, I was busy with career, and not in the mood to frolic with local nature. But late one evening during the Cherry Festival (a regional flirtation with mega tourism and heavy-duty partying), I arrived at the blue house from post-show revelry only to throw open the back door and discover the kitchen so thoroughly trashed that I thought a resentful student had given vent to feelings about a final grade. Either that or a straight-up break in. But even as I stood stock still in that doorway, telltale signs suggested a different invasion.

The trash had been tipped, sorted, scattered with an abandon unknown even to humans who are not particular about tidiness. Every moldy coffee filter and stale lettuce leaf looked as if it had been examined and then discarded across the linoleum floor. Every dirty dish had been slid from the counter, dropped nonchalantly, and licked clean. From the economy pack on the table, each Lorna Doone had been fully consumed, leaving a veneer of stickiness and—this was the worst—a Godiva chocolate bar had been beaten to smithereens and eaten alive. Only the shredded golden wrapper remained. The mess in my kitchen was bigger than the federal deficit.

Then I heard them. Lordy, they were still on the premises. In multiples.

Yes, in the bathroom, in my tub with the leaking faucet where, yes, I realized with some consternation, they could wash up together. After the feasting, these creatures were fastidious about washing. How polite. How many were there? I could hear their mutterings and growls, and then, as they realized I was there, they went silent. I crept down the hallway to peak through the door jamb into the bathroom tub. A plump mother and four kits were bathing in my tub. An entire effing nursery.

I backed off, propped open the screen door, grabbed a broom which I figured would be good enough weaponry, and marched through the back rooms of the house, singing at my loudest decibel level an off-key version of "You've Got a Friend." The kits moved fast; they were still small, and as soon as they hit the hallway, I could skid them into the living room, and out the front door like pucks on ice. Mistake. The mama raccoon, who had stayed behind, couldn't tell where her babies had gone, and only knew the tall predator was in her field of vision. As I circled again and prodded her toward the front door, she transformed. Became a woman warrior in a fighting pose—what had I done with her young? Rising on her back feet, she came to her full height, assumed the pose of a mother Terminator, a female Rambo on steroids. It stopped me cold. And in that moment, I realized I was dressed in a very short skirt, bare-legged with high, glitz-heeled sandals, and I had no idea where my phone was.

She hissed. She was pissed. She was going to eat me for dessert. She was not kidding.

And in that rare moment, face to face with this ferocious creature right in my living room, I knew a vulnerability I had kept at bay. Beyond the neighbor's shooting range, beyond the four-wheelers rushing the swamps down the road, beyond the snowstorms and the flooded garage, it comes to me. This encounter with a creature half my size, but who could assume a stance twice her norm, who bared her teeth and uttered menace, who had claws that matched Jack Sparrow's knives, this all could have been made easier with two. How nice it would be to have some help.

I backed away. She came toward me, growling, strutting on her hind legs, fur blooming like an explosion.

Yes, help was needed, not just help to cajole this angry mother out the front door, but help with the garage, the garden, negotiating the world—what I needed was assistance in the daily adventure. Someone to stand beside me during raccoon trouble. Someone else with a broom in hand.

Love, romance, lilacs—all of it was lovely. Love blooms from the clichés of those beginnings. Love rises from those roots and if you are patient, it sticks, as this one was. But what about this nest, now invaded? What about the guys next door who now had repeating rifles and a stock pile of ammo? For all that raccoons are plain wild, this mama, and now this place, forces me to reconsider the romance in light of a practical element.

What if there were a person who could share the joy and the toil? On top of that, this petty, annoying idea that just perhaps I wasn't as badass as I wanted to be. Maybe vulnerability would be ok, at least temporarily. Perhaps there could be love, romance, and also help. Perhaps help would make life less confrontive, less likely to be an awkward stand-off with Godiva-thieving masked bandits—let alone the neighbor guys, the roof, the snow plowing. Perhaps one does not need to wield the broom all alone. Perhaps love could include asking for help, or even moving to be with the one who could shove the raccoon safely out onto the porch, turn off the light, and take you to bed.

How We Knew

What could be wrong with living in a city for a while? Not that cities don't have their own form of wildness, but something else had become clear. We wanted to be together. So I moved. And for a while it worked. You know the truth, you know how it had to go.

We were married in the old-school library of the north shore Armour Estate, (of the Armour Chicago meat-packing family), an Italianate mansion with more crown filigree than cathedrals, with pleasure pools now filled with soil and perennials that still flowered in the spring. Today's more tender ears would be offended by the Armour advertising jingle, *Armour hot dogs, the dogs kids love to eat.* You've got to be kidding?

But their library was of a different architecture. Dark oak shelves held hundreds of old first editions from *Moby Dick* to *The Great Gatsby*, and every Harvard Classic ever printed. The room was available the day after Valentine's Day for a small wedding of thirty people that swelled to forty-five with the crashers, old friends who would not be denied. A local judge whose name we would promptly forget conducted the civil service and seemed overwhelmed by the champagne and strawberries we served before the wedding and all the chocolate that came after. There is an ongoing argument about whether the judge had slipped the word "obedient" into the vows when I had requested that not be included. Some guests claim they heard it. We did not. It was a good beginning, complete with songs around the piano. After that, we settled in to teaching at a boarding school on the north shore. It should have been enough. But city life with art and museums and theater and sushi and excellent wine only went so far if you came from a place where you have named the trees in your yard, where you once measured space in miles and acres, not blocks and streets.

For some, the sounds of the city are a song that draws them in and gives them a center. For me, only for so long, a couple years of apartment nesting, and then the migration had to turn. Yes, there was the sweet man—that's a binding unlike any other—but then there were these roots, now bare, pulled from my original soils. Finally, the noise of heavy traffic, of semis unloading, of rush hour, all overwhelmed me, and no matter how much culture ran alongside the noise, no matter how much I loved the ethnic food trucks in the square—none of it tied my heart to the place. The thing that bothered me most was how much money permeated the north shore—how the affluence became oppressive in size, so large it masked the real poverty tucked into the back streets, secreted in the tract houses. I was not living in a real world.

We were fine, he and I, but the place, the place was a poor fit.

Once herons bow to each other, the next thing that happens is they build a nest. But I couldn't find the right place, not there.

* * *

David spreads a map of Leelanau County on the kitchen counter of our Chicago apartment. It crackles with newness but opens its blue and green topography to the light. There it is, this sweet county, the little finger of Michigan's wide mitten. A peninsula from a peninsula. Leelanau is a word that people will tell you means sweet air, but it doesn't, it's made up, the way you have to make up a place in the world for yourself. I stand next to David, looking at the map, tracing the two-lane blue highway of M-22: Empire, Glen Arbor, Leland, Northport, Omena, Suttons Bay. Small towns surrounded by farms, open land, and rivers. And all of them bordered by Lake Michigan.

David's hand slides down my back and he rubs the low tight muscles, the twisted vertebra that have plagued me for so many months. His fingers gently turn against the hard knots. We've tried everything. Heat treatment. Ice. Chiropractors. But nothing seems to bring ease as much as his touch.

That summer, we had planned a trip out West to the great parks—Glacier, Yosemite, Bryce Canyon, ending in Grand Canyon—to finally see some big country. We were trying to figure out if we could afford it, if my back would take sleeping in a tent, how many miles of a "challenge" hike we could manage. We were looking forward to traveling with each other again. The heron's adventure, this time paired.

The phone had rung innocently enough. Norm. Our friend in Leelanau County, Michigan. Up north. His neighbors were looking for house sitters for six weeks for the summer. Leelanau? Are you kidding? We loved Leelanau County, and being near old friends like Norm and Mimi would mean renewal of an old friendship. Travel? Next year, the parks. Instead, we packed for a north country house in the woods.

I should have known then.

During that first week in a borrowed home, I watched the dappled light of trees drift across a green yard and realized how deeply we were sleeping without the sound of the inter-state wafting through the windows. As we sat in the cool sun of Michigan's June mornings, we felt a freeing of thought—a drifting into a wider lens. After the deep commitment to creating an urban life rich with culture and the demands of career, the mood inside our days began to shift toward self-care: walking the dunes, reading deeply, studying the gardens. Yes, we were planning for the school year, but at night, we stared at the stars we were learning to name—unmarred by ambient light. Simple things like collecting Petoskey stones shouldn't change a body, but here in the gentle bending to pick up the fossil, in the examination of the patterns, they do. There occurred an accumulation of gratitude that was slowly, unerringly, turning sticky as pine gum, turning into longing, then attachment.

We began to study the history of the county, to learn about the original Anishinaabe peoples, the occupation of the land—not easy to accept. We learned the myths of the Sleeping Bear and turtle island, learned the story of ship-wrecks and the Life Saving efforts, the slow settlement, and the long history of human interface with the waters of the bays and the Manitou channel.

We were falling in love with the place.

* * *

Early morning. We are climbing a high dune that holds a view of other dunes, Little Glen Lake, several beaches and settlement farms. I stand in a warm wind blooming through the sand blowout behind me. The air on my skin teaches me how the current works, how the wind warms as it moves over sand. The distant view fills me up, and I realize how many places I can already name, even at this distance—some native names, some settlement. I pour the second cup of coffee from the thermos and we sit on the edge of the sand bluff. David balances his cup on his knee and slurps off the top. We study the morning light as it hollows itself with day. I can feel the silence seeping into me and into David, who is a quiet man, but whose deeper calm is returning with each gentler hour.

He leans over and whispers into my shoulder, "I think we should talk to a realtor."

To make a dream into something real is a bumpy road. We did talk to realtors, and finally picked one, a tall man with a radio voice and wry humor, and a willingness to work with our limited budget. Even if we sold my house—which I wasn't sure I could, we were teaching for private schools— lower salaries and fewer benefits than public schools. We were privileged yes, we knew that, and tried to compensate by being socially conscious, but we were not rich by any stretch. After looking at many lots and parcels and plots with John Martin, only two were affordable and held our interest. Two pieces that might suit us.

But we couldn't decide.

We'd visited both places with John, the realtor. We'd gone back alone. We'd been back and forth between them so many times that each visit only came to confuse us more. We needed advice, not from the realtor, but from friends who knew us and knew the county, people who had already lived in this place, who could say something about the logistics, the proximity, the weather. Who could speak of the ghosts and the heart of the place.

* * *

We pack cookies and a thermos of strong tea "corrected" with brown liquor, all of it into our now battered Jeep and we drive to Norm and Mimi's house. Since we've taken the top off the Wrangler, we wrap our friends in blankets and bundle them into a wind-rushed back seat, and drive out into the cool. First stop, ten acres on Wheeler road, a steep west-facing slope with a small plot of pines in front, wooded in back. We pull in, climb out, and walk over the summer flora. There are lovely trees half way up the ridge, an awkward but level spot for a camp or house (in some far distant future), a lower contour for a garden. The land would have little morning light, but heavy afternoon light, making it a warm lot. There was western light, the idea of sunsets, a low valley spread out before us.

We spend an hour there. We talk about it. Mimi reminds me that we would be close to Glen Arbor, a lively tourist town surrounded by innumerable summer cottages and newer homes, a town with good restaurants and shops. But expensive. Norm nods, tells us this land is a good lot for a decent price. Space, trees, light, a valley. Warm.

Then we load up again, and in the now waning light, we head for Lake View Orchards. This is the plot we hadn't expected. We are not really fans of associations, but this one consists of large lots, all a minimum of ten acres, and is the site of a former orchard. In fact, instead of pine trees, this parcel supports five acres of cherry trees. The rest is forest of mixed hardwoods, and somewhere, so the brochure had said, a seasonal lake view. This one is a high lot, acres above ravines, and the one clearing where a house can be built is deep in berry brambles. There is a stateliness to the trees that draws upward the eyes, the mind. There are ash, birch, maples and the smooth-barked beech, my favorites because they become hollow hosts for everything that needs to live inside a tree. David teases me, "Just widow makers. Fall down in a good windstorm." We walk and talk and drink the tea. Mimi tells us that Empire, the village a mile away, is more blue-collar than Glen Arbor, with fewer shops, two bars but only one with decent food. Then she pauses. She tells me the village has a lovely library. A library. Fate stirs my secret needs.

When do we find the marker tree? As we walk the boundaries. On what would be the southwest border of the lot. A marker tree is a tree bent deliberately so it grows into the shape of a chair without a back leg, so it "points" in a direction, but it's still a living tree. In this case, it points south across the orchard toward the small protected lake, Taylor Lake, deep in the national park. Marker trees were like signposts, made by the hunting peoples before us. The Anishinaabe have been here. To find one on this plot seems like, well, a very special sign, a request for reverence, but also an added responsibility, a suggestion on how to steward the land—take care of the trees. Follow their path. Can we do that?

Norm stands at the top of the ravine and looks down. "With all these trees, you know, gonna be cool here. Feel it?" We stand at the brink of the ravine and the lake air, already chilled, is scented with gully and root. A cool place.

David walks around restlessly. He has to pee. So does Norm. They walk into the woods. It's contagious, now I have to pee. Mimi and I walk the other way, into the trees, squat briefly in the ferns. We meet again in the clearing.

"Well, that does it." Norm says.

We drive out through the orchards, and I don't know if a decision has been made or not. But after we drop Norm and Mimi home, David turns into the scenic outlook on Benzie Trail. From there, we can actually see in the far distance the rise where the orchard once thrived, where the marker tree still lives, old as it is.

"How's your back?" he asks, reaching for me.

All evening, through all the climbing in the rough woods, through the walking over rough terrain, I have not noticed. "Fine," I smile.

And then he asks, "Warm or cool?"

And I think deeply, and I know he is right to ask this way. One will be easier than the other, one will be warmer than the other. Warm or cool?

And I choose. "Cool"

"Cool then." He smiles, and I know that was his choice as well.

We choose the harder land to work, the one with a marker tree that points to water and mystery, the one with the darker history and greater responsibility, where spring will come late. The one with the hidden lake view that we will choose not to reveal, the one that will burden us with caretaking an orchard, the one that will ask that we remember, as best we can, the indigenous peoples, one that will make me bend my back again to land as I have all my life. Despite what may cause pain, I choose cool. When we tell Norm, he laughs and says he knew already. "You peed on that lot. You marked territory."

I think about this. I know enough history to know that land is never really ours to possess, or anybody's for that matter, that claiming "territory" is a word laced with colonial and unjust history. But maybe, just maybe, in going through the rituals of purchasing and caretaking, we can touch stewardship, touch the way knowing a place can point, like a marker tree, to a way of life given to reverence.

Where the Music Rises

How we find home, make home, is not simple. What I know now: one must do so as the bird builds a nest, and one must also be open to ways that the place will claim you. An active process. We now owned a parcel under contract, complete with the marker tree, but we weren't sure what to do with it. Hold it, build on it? We were still committed to jobs in Chicago and would be for several years. How would Leelanau claim us? Otherwise, we would become what the locals call with dread, "summer people."

My back had ached every morning since we'd signed. It was not just the money; my muscles seemed to tighten with decision-making. Am I am one of those people who cannot live without pain because I am never confident of my own knowing?

But the summer was still there too, full of its own life. And in that life, the small town of Cedar hosts a Polka Fest in July of every summer. A polka fest, a long-standing, wildly loud, often drunken festival that draws polka lovers from all over the state, and honors the Polish ancestry of the families who settled here. For those days, this village in the center of the county becomes the hub of the universe. They say you can, on a clear night, hear the polka beat on Sugar Loaf Mountain, ten miles away. The bands arrive from all over the country and play for three days. It is a raucous and proud marathon of polka-dom.

That weekend, I am too uncomfortable to dance, and am trying just to stay with the daily routines, but David says, "Let's go, just to listen." He's feeling his heron, his wanderlust. We had been stunned by our decision to purchase the lot, stunned by our change of direction, stunned by the very idea of owning property, and now we were going to attend the Polka Festival in Cedar?

If we were to become locals, this would be a start.

As young as we are, we both grew up in places where the old polka ways thrived, and we both love the charm of the polka with its toe-tapping spirit and driving old-world accordion. So we drive the back roads to Cedar and park in the baseball diamond's outfield, pay the nominal entry, join the crowds under a white tent half the size of a football field. I sit at a long makeshift table, drink a dark beer with bitter foam, eat sausage and cabbage laced with caraway and rye.

In that dust-laden air, older women with their solid bodies dressed in out-of-fashion shirt-waist dresses or ruffled skirts lift their feet and take the snuffling steps as easily as if they were ballerinas, swinging in wide and giddy turns under a big man's arms—a grace belied by size. Women far younger than I am, purple hair shining, dance freely in their strappy dresses; young men in rock-band tees kick their heels in a step that isn't a polka but honors the beat. Kids under ten leap in and pretend to breakdance to polka rhythms, and grown-old men join in a circle, arm-in-arm, holding each other up, and launch a kick-step that harkens back to the great crossing over. I stare in admiration.

Then David is standing before me, and into my feet enters the beat of the Beer Barrel Polka, its irresistible shuffle and leap, and he takes my hand, lifts me up and pulls me out onto the sturdy board floor where the circle of human sweat and laughter whirls, defying age and bad backs. It is there, in the old music, under the tent in a remote village in Northern Michigan, at a Polka Fest, that I feel it happen. A slow claim is being made. As I turn to join a circle, I put into a different place that easy access to theater and museums and art galleries and niche bookstores and ethnic restaurants. Looking into the plain and ruddy faces of the ordinary elders who come to polka, I feel *among them*. They are welcoming me with their bitter beer, their sausage and cabbage. And here, I suddenly know: I want to lose my youth, let my nails chip and my hair gray. I pick up my feet and defy pain. I twirl in David's arms and we step into the parade, process the circle with "Jim and the Umpa Dudes" pounding down the beat and we dance until they call time at two o'clock in the morning. We are hot and drenched, dusty and sore, but despite the beer, we are not drunk; we are thrillingly uplifted, and we drive slowly home, windows down, the night-cool air drying the sweat on our faces.

The next morning, my back doesn't hurt. The place has begun the process of laying claim—with every ritual I attend, I am becoming of them, for this too is a "returning to," to land and places that open like corn to sun. I can hear polka music from anywhere in the universe, but I hear it best in Leelanau, where it first laid claim. My back doesn't hurt again all summer.

Ghost Orchard

We had purchased land with five acres of an orchard.

The day they pulled out the cherry trees, we stopped calling our property by the association's name, Lake View Orchards, and secretly began to call it Ghost Orchard. When the trees were gone, we felt the change in terrain. What we didn't expect was a change in our interior terrain—how when we change the land or adjust a view, we are also changing and adjusting a view within ourselves

People speak of certain houses "with a view." Realtors advertise sites for homes with "lake view" or sites with a "big west view." The play, *Six Rms Riv Vu*, capitalized on a city apartment view. Large or small, urban or rural, the landscape is what you see from a certain point of view. If you live in a city as we did for several years, the view may be the slice of street or alley that tells you about traffic, temperature, and your neighbor's temperament. If you move to a more rural setting, it may consist of what you can see standing at the brow of a wide sloping meadow.

The summer we purchased property in Lake View Orchards, a former cherry farm in Leelanau County, our five-acre slice of the four-hundred some tart trees on our land carried a bumper crop. As the crop ripened, we often walked in the orchard, brushing against those laden trees. The trees had not been sprayed that year, and thus the huge crop was probably a stress crop, so that year the fruit was pure. It was likely the last year the trees would bear. We invited our friends to come and take as much as they could. We spent long days in the orchard, picking among the shadows of the trees. I learned how the old orchard spread like a palm through the mixed hardwoods on this high plateau. Though our acreage was only a small part of the original six-hundred acre farm, I walked the entire farm, trying to understand the orchard. I was in a kind of grief for those trees.

The trees had to go. We'd received notice from the Department of Agriculture. We'd talked with the soil conservation officer. "The trees are diseased. They won't last long now that the manager has stopped spraying. We've already had complaints from the neighboring farmers. You'll need to take them out." I remembered that tart cherry trees are chemically dependent. They are designer trees bred for high yield, but susceptible to all kinds of blights and pests. They can't live long without the fertilizer and pesticides. These pests can spread miles to other orchards, so that five acres (and the surrounding abandoned orchard) was a threat to the other orchards in the area, the entire local economy. That first winter, when we received the letter from the officials, we were also grappling with our ignorance. We had done the research; we just didn't have the skills or the will to farm the trees. We'd also learned that the land had been supporting orchards for nearly eighty years, and the soil was badly depleted. And perhaps poisoned—it had been an orchard through the DDT and Malathion eras. This was the turning point. If we were to be good stewards, yes, this was the time to remove the orchard and rest this piece of working earth.

But nothing prepared me for the death of the orchard. One chill March morning John Stanz's Excavating crew rolled up and began removing our four-hundred trees and several thousand of our neighbors' trees. It was not pretty; it was not easy. It was dirty—the mangling of each tree out of the old soil. I cringed all day as the big yellow claw yanked these slim, leafless trunks up by the roots. Though the machine was efficient and quick, nothing soothed my unease as I watched them take the orchard, damaged and compromised as it was. I wondered if trees, even such domesticated ones as the tart cherry, have ghosts. Would these trees haunt us? I wondered how long before I would walk the land and not see the trees in my mind, not miss them. It was then that David and I renamed our parcel Ghost Orchard—half in humor, half in reverence for the lost orchard. We knew this was a good thing for the land. We also knew that any tree is a living thing, doing its work in its own way.

So out of that reverence, we tried not to be wasteful. We cut away the roots, then the tops, stacking the whole trunks to dry. They are not thick, but they could be stripped and planked for trim in a someday house. This much we could do. But even this could not erase my sadness as, on a cool day spackled with clouds, we watched the shattered branches burn.

How do we learn to see differently?

I am looking away from the rising smoke and dark crackle, across the now empty, open field. From where I stand on the corner of our section, I see a high front moving in from the lake. I am reminded that sun and rain will touch this Earth in ways that it hasn't for decades. The old soil will be rinsed again.

For the first time, I notice the unbroken wholeness of the field. As I walk away from the flames, I feel a "knowing" arrive slowly. The west winds, riding over the Empire bluffs and across this open area, must have kept the frost from settling. And then I see it. With the orchard gone, the view emerges. Looking north, I see all the way to a wind barrier of poplar trees on the far side. I see into a topography of ravines and moraines. I feel the contours of the section, its shape. Turning to the cardinal points, I see what my father meant when he talked about the *lay of land*. The land feels wider, and more—I search for the word—more possible. With this raw look at its structure, the bare bones of the hillsides, the question turns: what does the land need? How do we care for it? This new view casts a spell—widening my thinking: what is it I see when I see a long way. Perhaps it is seeing a longer way that helps me think in longer ways. A viewspell.

Though I've never seen their ghosts, I do miss the trees. But with this new openness, I realize their absence has evoked change. There are things to do for this space, this soil, new trees to plant, and perhaps native grasses, wildflowers. But the soil itself—it will rest first. We will walk through the view.

Outhouse Endearments

Building an outhouse is not what I expected to do with my last days of freedom before returning to work in Chicago, not what I expected to do with any moment of my life. Digging through hardpan to frame a four-foot hole or measuring the height and opening for a toilet seat—these were not experiences I would have selected for the last precious days of summer light. It is our first building, our first real stake in the soil. It was also the last place I expected to gain an insight into how this kind of work might go. Though I have done manual labor all my life, I have never done construction. I have not swung hammers for a living, never pounded nails. I do not know the language.

Though we had vowed to disturb this land as little as possible, it became obvious we needed an outhouse while we camped on this land, while deciding what to do with these acres. One can't go around digging holes behind trees forever. Three of us—David, Norm, and I joined for outhouse duty. Both of these men have built their own homes with their own calloused hands. I have built a glue-only birdhouse. But I am willing and able; I have those broad palms. I say, "Just give me good directions." They promise.

These are men who like women, respect women, and will give even a birdhouse woman a chance to build an outhouse. What surprises me is the way they talk about this building process using terms of endearment: *honey, sweetheart, darling,* words I have disliked because they are patronizing, objectifying, or belittling. The only exception: my father could call me *Baby.* Because he changed my diapers, held me as I spat up on him, he'd earned the right. But there are no terms of endearment that I can welcome from others. And Norm and David don't; they know better. But here they are, calling the half-built outhouse by these terms of endearment.

Like this. As they rough out the drawings and list lumber and nails they will need, they tell me this outhouse is *a love* of a design, a *beauty* of a plan. During the digging, they say it's "gonna be a sweetie." Mitered corners become "darlins," a bird's mouth becomes a "sweetheart." When the building process begins, and we are cutting and laying out the walls, they call it "love," or they comfort the work—*easy, easy*—as they line up the studs, grinning and shaking their heads in appreciation.

Then I notice what happens among the three of us. They play with our own names. David becomes Davey, Mr. D, Big D, The Earl, after his last name Early. Norm becomes Normy, El Normal, Big Wheel, even Stormin' Norman or simply Storm. I am called by my initials at first, AMO—a nickname David gave me long ago, then Spamo, then the oldest and most disliked of puns, The Omen. "Tell The Omen she should use the nail gun." For once, I don't object, especially since using the nail gun is an act of trust, an honor of sorts. I see that what they do is not the same as objectifying. It's not the same as the patronizing *oh honey* in a mansplaining situation. It's an odd form of nomination, this moniker of shortening, varying, like an honorific. As I measure the width of the seat for a bottom, I understand that this practice is not about sexism or superiority, but rapport.

I do ask them, "*Why the nicknames?*" as they measure and cut the plywood. The response comes slowly, in between setting the lap and king studs, holding a wall plumb and hammering.

Norm says, "People say men don't talk to each other. That's not true. When I turn a name, I'm saying I appreciate you. It's a small way of offering attention." Later, after the top plate is in place, David tells me, "Calling the building 'sweet' encourages the work. We're aware of how hard it is to work together and stay easy."

I ask them if this happens on all projects. "If the crew is getting along," David says. "It stays off the tension."

The walls of the outhouse are up. We start on the rafters of the small shed roof. It takes some scrambling up and down a ladder. It takes some overhead lifting. It takes some heart to stay with it. The trees all around rustle in the slow breeze that is not cool. But it goes well. *Oh dolly.*

I remember how I have reacted to people who have called me "sweetheart" or the "Bad Omen." Often, terms of endearment seem to be used whiningly instead of winningly—a way of manipulating. Sometimes nicknames seem to cover insult rather than encouragement. "My name is..." I correct them briskly. If pressed, I explain no nickname or endearment measures up to the sound of my own name spoken with friendliness or regard. That is still true, but I also see, as we begin to hinge the secondhand door on this small, necessary building, that I have missed a component. Depending on the tone and circumstances, a nickname might represent the same sense of appreciation my given name does, and endearments might best be used when applied to a process like building, even an outhouse. The words are not innately incorrect, but rather the way that they are used makes the difference, the attitude, the application creates nuance.

After tar paper, the shingles are handed up and tacked into place, and the seat is sanded so the rim of the hole is smooth enough not to leave splinters in someone's ass. Meanwhile, sweating and smelling like a garage, I am slopping old motor oil on the plywood's exterior so the porcupines won't eat it. We all finish at the same time, crack the cold beers from the truck cooler, and step back. We look admiringly at one small outhouse, as proud as if we had built a mansion. Norm picks up the last bit of two-by-four—all that is left from the building supplies. They have measured down to the foot—there is no waste. Pun intended. But what he says as he opens the door, "Now that's a honey of a john." This is the beginning of building; this is the start of what I must learn to do if I am to have a home. I will learn to strike a nail cleanly, to measure accurately, to accept and deliver terms of endearment, to honor the work with a touch of play and affection.

Wishbones and Scars

When I was a child, our family couldn't afford icicles for the Christmas tree so my mother saved coffee can ribbons, the metal strip you peeled off with a key when you opened the can. And then, on Thanksgiving Day, to divert and appease us, and to satisfy our wish that Christmas (in our minds the real holiday) would come sooner, my mother gave us these flat spools of tin from the cans and told us to pull them into curly metal ribbons which would serve as icicles for the tree. My sister and I were so charmed and enthused about the project that we both cut ourselves on the sharp edges. To this day, one of our Thanksgiving traditions is to look for the scars. If we look closely, we believe we find tiny lines where the metal once tore our palms. My sister says it's good luck to have these scars, and after years of watching her make happiness from unexpected materials, I believe her and often make wishes on those tiny lines.

For me, the whole month of November is like that family story, full of contrasts and unexpected composition, an over-exposed black and white photograph. Thanksgiving itself is a holiday of the double negative, shadowed by its own troubled past, its legacy of appropriation and colonialism. Its history relies on a "misinformed" American romanticism, and if that history is examined deeply, there exist as many holes as stakes to claim. Many Americans are not aware that the supposed 1621 "First Thanksgiving" is a faintly refer-enced (only two documents refer to it) and deeply exoticized mythology; they take it on whole-cloth, filling in gaps with an imagined kumbaya spirit. That said, in recent years, more of us now acknowledge the facts: it wasn't until George Washington set up a day of thanks giving in November 1789 that anything like a Thanksgiving holiday was noted at all, and only after Abraham Lincoln made it a federal holiday smack-dab in the middle of the Civil War (1863) did it take on some of the dimensions it holds today. Since then, it has gradually become the secular holiday most related to family. That was the case in my childhood: despite the scars, despite the misinformed history. It was family time despite a troublesome history.

How I have resolved these contradictions, inadequately and likely in full denial, is to view it as a harvest festival of gratitude, which in some cultures and in some countries, it may have been. Thus, in the paradox of a false past, the complexities of right and wrong continue, a scar we white Americans carry with us.

Those complexities reflect the month as well: Novem-ber's skeletal trees against soft smoke from first fires, its lonely early snows against warm homecomings, harvest's final throes against the approaching Advent, deer season's tale-telling failures against Christmas anticipation, too-heavy sweaters and hot cider, too-cold nights and too much spiced wine. All contradictories. And I suppose that for this Thanksgiving, our decision, David's and mine, plays into this feeling as well. We have decided at last. We have shared the news with my parents. On a rare clear night with northern lights scattering our skies, we have told them we will marry.

And so, as is our tradition—despite the contradictions, my four siblings and I drive long hours to one of our homes. We hold to the family ritual because we care for each other, and this time, I have news to share. Ironically, once we've arrived, there are so many of us with so many children, we rarely get a chance to talk deeply. But over the years, just from rubbing against each other's lives, we have composed unique rites. For example, the smells of our Thanksgivings. Rather than traditional sage dressing, we stir in apples from the backyard tree, the one Dad says has been there since God, a tree so old he doesn't know its kind, just that it's a cooking apple which farmers once cherished but no longer grow. Nothing depicts contrast like that dressing—sweet old apples and sharp onion.

My sister and I, helping our proud mother as much as she will let us, cook giblets separately, and before dinner, we pull out brothy pieces as a kind of appetizer. Slicing the heart, we peak through the chamber holes as though they were windows into each other's hearts before dripping the thin salty slices onto our tongues. That sliced open heart, that taking in.

At dinner our family sits down in disorder: no Norman Rockwell image of quiet charm and quaint affection with our Thanksgiving. Not even enough serenity to get through grace before rowdy noise dominates our platters, primarily because a dozen grandchildren under twelve vie for space and drumsticks. Some child doesn't like the cranberry Jell-O—*looks like blood*: some other wants only potatoes—*sorry kid, put some green on that plate.* There are small avoidances in the conversations, and there are controversies revealed—*Yes, it's true, we will not invite any cousins to our wedding. It will be small.*

Small, with this family?

But as this harvest meal ends in pie and disarray, one tradition holds. The family who hosted the previous year's dinner brings the wishbone from last year's turkey wrapped in an old linen napkin. Then the hosts for the current year's dinner unwrap it, make a wish, and break the bone. This year it is my parents' turn to make the wish, and I wonder if, when the rotation comes around to them again, they will be able to host. My mother picks up the bone as children swarm around her.

"Grandma, grandma, what's your wish?" they beg to know. She closes her eyes. For a moment it is as though she holds her life in her hands.

"I can't tell," she says. I am surprised. Often this wish has been an opportunity to congratulate or give thanks for a recent birth, a new job, an impending (or in my case) or better marriage. I suspect—is this egocentric?—that their wishes may have to do with David and me, with their hopes. Their disappointments. I have the dubious honor of being the only divorcee in the family, and now I am to marry again. They love me, but they know. I am a pigeon-heron, not necessarily reliable. And this man? His family is Presbyterian—what to do with that?

"It won't come true if we tell," Dad agrees with her. The little ones turn silent, puzzling over this idea. Their secret then—to keep the peace?

Then my parents' lift their old fingers, swollen but firm, and grasp each tine of the wishbone. They know to put their thumbs up, knuckles together, and to make sure they twist their wrists just so. Each aged hand pulls gently away from the other. The kids watch, the bone spreads, and finally, with a quick crack, it shatters. But this time, in a wild wish of its own will, both prongs of the breastbone break, and the paddle bone flips through air, flying across plate and table, banging against the window as though it still wanted to be a bird, not a wish. Nothing like this has ever happened.

The children are awed. "How did you do that?"

"Do it again."

Like a startled flock of birds, nervous laughter rises, wonder and worry combined. My father chuckles, picks his teeth with his bone. With a sadder smile, my mother fondles the part she has in her fingertips. A grandchild comes to her knees and asks plaintively, "Does it still happen?"

"What, child?" My mother is caught in her own thoughts.

"The wish. Does the wish still come true?"

"Oh, I don't know." She answers softly. In her answer, the contradictions roll on. The child wanders away. My sister goes to the windowsill, rummages among the African violets and comes up with the errant piece. She turns it in her palms against the place where the coffee can cut her palm—a token of the broken.

"Here's the wish," she says and walks across the room. I think she will give the little coin-shaped bone to one of my parents, and it crosses my mind that if I could give one of them their wish, I wouldn't know which one to choose. But my sister brings the keepsake to me, looks me straight in the eye, and drops it into my hand, my own nest of scars.

"Make a wish," she says, smiling.

No one will ever know what the original wish was to be. I need to make my own wish. See through to my own heart. And I do. I wish for light, for this Michigan winter to be easy on us—that for all the contrasts and composi-tions and stories and histories that may or may not be true, we manage to be in one another's presence for a while, in gratitude now. For this is to be a time of going forward with awareness and wonder. This is to be a time of new and renewed commitment.

Outside, like a curtain coming down on an old story, a new snow sheers the oak trees with fine and lovely lace.

In Search of a Small Plan

As a child, I was swept away by the opulent film *The Philadelphia Story*. I announced that I wanted to live in that big house. As I stood on the family farmhouse's sloping back porch that was badly in need of a paint job, I imagined huge rooms with white pillars and ornate trim. "And chandeliers as big as tables," I claimed, throwing my arms wide, only to bang my knuckles on a rickety screen door.

Handing me a broom, my mother asked quietly, tiredly, "Do you need a house that big? Think about what you really need."

That statement, over the years, has become haunting.

David and I, until now, have been happily nomadic. Since our marriage, we've lived in two apartments in Chicago, and since our return to Northern Michigan, several rented houses. Small and efficient. We relished finding ways to make our eclectic mix of antique and discount furniture fit into oddly shaped spaces. We bought carpet pieces and cut them to fit one house, then cut them again to fit a different room in a different house, until finally they became the mats in a mud room. We arranged and rearranged artwork, putting up and leaving out according to the wall size. We changed our hearts a little every time we moved, and that kept them nimble. We grew, shifted, played with the spaces we found ourselves in.

But when it comes to books, being nomadic lost its charm.

One day I needed a book that hadn't been and couldn't be unpacked because we didn't have enough shelf space. It was in a box, and those boxes were piled ten high in some corner of some storage space somewhere in the county. When I can't have books, hundreds of books, close at hand, something goes awry in my life. This time, it was simple drama. I burst into tears, "I can't find the Nikki Giovanni poems." I was working my way toward hysteria. It was not just that book. The week before I hadn't been able to find my favorite tree encyclopedia, and before that I'd had to go to the library for a reference text of which I had two copies packed somewhere in another buried box. My tears were a culmination. I bawled, "Before I die, I want a room with enough bookshelves for every book I have, and all the ones I will ever have. Before I die!" I blew my nose unceremoniously and closed my eyes, seeing the space, seeing the room surrounding me. Windows and books. Light and words. That was what I wanted. But by then my tissue was in shreds, and I had a deadline to meet. No time for hysteria.

The next day, as we finish coffee in the too-small kitchen of a house located on the campus where we are teaching, David sets his cup down, and leans in. "We could build."

"Bookshelves? Where?" The place is packed.

"A house. With enough bookshelves for all the books until you die."

A house?

* * *

We had originally hoped to renovate an older home, but we had found that ten acres of land. Or maybe it found us. The parcel, near the village of Empire and our beloved Sleeping Bear Dunes National Lakeshore, included mixed hardwoods on the edge of a lush ravine. White birch and maple dotted the bluff. The privacy and light-shimmering canopy had lured us in, and the central clearing of brambles and weeds, probably created by lumber trucks during the last cutting, meant we would disturb few trees if we ever decided to build there. Still, it seemed a long way off, the very idea intimidating. And there was the idea of what we wanted, of how to be good stewards with our current resources and still build a place that would, of course, draw on new resources. How would we build gently, with integrity, in that lovely space, that brambled clearing with the dappled light?

We asked my mother's question: what do we really need?

We need room for the two of us to move easily, to welcome my stepson, and to entertain small groups of friends. We need a place to cozy up. We like efficiency, but we are not appliance hogs, and we don't have a lot of recreational toys—that means intimate rooms and a one-car garage. We need graceful light, proportionate lines, and interesting transitions within spaces. And a lot of bookshelves. Even though we had decided to build, we hoped to use as few resources as possible—not only because of our budget, but because new houses tax the environment.

We began by looking for a small plan with a focus on aesthetics, not square feet. We began by studying the land we had become stewards of. I remembered the American architect, Frank Lloyd Wright, built his Wisconsin studio, Taliesin East, on the "brow" of the hill so that it would blend into the contours of the land, not dominate it. (The word "Taliesin" means "shining brow.") As our search evolved, we knew only that it must be a smaller home (1000 and 1200 square feet) that would fit into the "brow" of our hillside, would look natural to the contours. Could we find a design that worked with the drop in elevation? Could we tuck the house into the hillside so it would have an organic look?

Why small? Especially when we considered several thousand books. Maybe because I remember growing up in a farmhouse with small, gabled, functional rooms that I shared with siblings. My sense of family was born in crowded hallways which doubled as toy rooms and a woodlot that replaced TV. Because those rooms were multi-purpose, we learned about sharing space and suspending territorialism. We learned about being together—not in perfect harmony—but in an imperfect, evolving sense of community. Despite childhood spats, I grew to love nearby voices, the close presence of another person. For me, small space meant communal bigness.

We began as many people do, by looking at design magazines and home catalogues. Many large floorplans offered interesting options, but few small ones revealed the artistic integrity for which we hungered, and not one depicted a one-car garage. We had hoped our need for a small home would have simplified the process. Instead, it created a greater challenge. I found myself confused by the choices, not being able to imagine a room with a door here, a window there, and where would we put my grandmother's buffet, our Mission-style table and chairs if the rooms were so small?

But as we searched, we began to learn more about ourselves and how we "practiced" home. For example, we loved to cook with friends, so we wanted a central stove with access to other spaces. We also wanted morning light, which meant an eastern exposure in that kitchen. But the hillside slope ran west, not east. And what about the bookshelves?

We sketched and resketched. We bought graph paper and tissue paper and a lot of erasers. We drank a lot of coffee and then a lot of brown liquor and then finally, late one night I ended up lying on the floor, spilling scotch over a dozen rough sketches and bad drawings and newsprint with little squares, hollering, "Where are the bookshelves?"

David leaned over and made one quiet suggestion before kissing me, "Maybe we need an architect."

I sat up (after the kiss). "An architect? Can we afford that?" Like I was buying a car.

* * *

An architect isn't the answer for everyone, but it was for us. With some hesitation, and after a good deal of research, we contacted an architect—not an easy decision for two independent people who are as thrift-minded as professional misers. However, in Don Wilson, we discovered a compassionate man who respected our wish to build only what we needed. We sat nervously in his Glen Arbor office, a small building with lots of light and a wide desk he had built himself. The place was not pretentious, not big. Don Wilson was older, a heavy smoker with a dark personality, but he listened carefully. He listened to stories of my childhood on the farm, my theater experience. He noted David's construction experience, and our attraction to the designs of Frank Lloyd Wright. He agreed to develop the working drawings (these are not full specifications for contracted builders, but briefer designs that were affordable) for a home of 1500 square feet, larger than we had first imagined, but his idea of interlocking rooms terraced down the ravine—starting with an east kitchen—answered our need for a place that fit the site, and convinced us.

In the process, he offered a remark that affirmed our search and sensibility. He exhaled deeply, "Small homes are challenging because it's easier to design big. Small ones call for art." When he said that, I felt every muscle in my back relax. A little domestic art. That's what we needed. And then he looked at me, "We'll find a place for all those books."

The last thing David told him—we had to be able to build it ourselves. We were going to go full-bore DIY. And that's when I really knew. We were in for the long haul. Whatever it meant to belong to a place, to steward and not possess, all of that meant we would do it ourselves. We would touch the land as lightly as possible, and we would build it with our own hands.

Old Beams

I didn't know wood, especially old wood, had a voice as evocative as our own.

In the new home we were building slowly and with immense care, we decided to use as much recycled material as we could, and in that process, to use the old beams from the last of the authentic barns on my family's farm. David and I had managed to save and store a dozen of those original beams—solid ten-by-ten white pine, immobile, and as heavy as steel. They had deep character from the ax-hewn marks, but they were also ungraded, having never seen the interior of a lumberyard. To use ungraded wood in a new house, it had to be tested. An engineer had looked at the plans, calculated the weight loads, and because the structure was unusual, these loads had to be tested on the actual lumber. Otherwise, no permits.

* * *

One hot August afternoon, David, our friend Norm, and I borrow a flatbed truck, loaded the beams, and drove north to Robert Foulkes' White Oak Timber Framing business on Lake Leelanau. With Robert's help, we could test for the point loads these beams would bear, the first step in the grading process.

We turn into his work yard, lumbering down a grassy slope to an open air, log-frame workshop. Around the dusty yard, men work with oak beams set on sturdy sawhorses, using special tools to create the mortise and tenons that hold together a timber frame structure. An old Dalmatian, "Blue," barks skeptically as we pile out of the cab. Other hounds rise from the shade and investigate the wheels of the flatbed.

Robert, an energetic man with intelligent eyes explains that our first step is to place each barn beam on blocks which are set apart the same distance as the beam will span in our house. On the beams he places a hydraulic cylinder with a steel plate balanced exactly where the point load will bear. With a forklift, he hoists a ten-by-sixteen white oak beam from the yard into his workshed, and balances it parallel above the old barn beams, then slowly lowers the oak beam so that it rests lightly on the steel plate of the hydraulic cylinder. This will become the immobile object. We tie the old beam to the new beam with truck straps. On each end of the old beam, we also tie a string line spanning the load. This will measure the deflection, how much each beam bends. Will it bend? Even if the beam holds, the deflection must fall within a safe range, or the beam won't pass the county codes. In the heat of the afternoon, the dust rises in his shed.

In the shade of the open-air barn, Robert climbs down from the forklift, makes a few adjustments, strolls casually over to the press of this hydraulic jack on steroids. He looks at us wryly, "You know if they aren't strong enough, you'll go home with kindling." I swallow hard. David nods. Norm shakes his head, sighing.

The dust swirls. Slivers of afternoon light fall among us through the pine siding.

Robert begins pumping the hydraulic lift. As it presses against the old beam, the new oak beam, balanced above it, remains immovable, but the old beam becomes the pressure point against which it presses. As Robert pumps, a gauge measures the number of pounds pressing onto our beam. We can see the numbers on the large dial. These numbers indicate the number of pounds that this beam would bear in our actual house.

One thousand pounds.

It is pure physics, a textbook lesson, but it is also more than that. It is the weight of a building which will house us, it is the need to connect with the farm where I had grown up, it is a way to reuse material and to honor the original giant trees that had grown a hundred years ago in some forest nearby, but now gone.

I watch them work over these last dregs of the barn that housed my childhood. I didn't want to be sentimental, but I wanted with my whole heart for the beams to hold, to be strong, and yet, how could this hundred-year-old wood stand up to this pressure?

Two thousand pounds and rising.

The workmen, attracted by our silence and the suspense, move in to watch.

Ton and a half.

A wise looking older man named Sam snaps pictures.

Two tons.

The dogs, sensing a great question in their humans, trot nervously around the circle.

I listen, watching. At the first sound, I look around. It is an eerie, high-pitched humming. I don't know who is singing. Then, the source. The beams have voices.

At five thousand pounds, the first beam begins to creak, a high note of slow protest, and this continues with operatic steadiness until eight thousand pounds when it evolves into a continuous high moan. Robert stops pumping, "Sometimes, they make this sound before they break"

He says, "Stand back."

He says, "Wait."

If it holds for ten minutes, he will increase the pressure. We wait. The men shuffle. The dogs sniff. Minutes pass and the wind dusts its way quietly into the barn.

Nothing happens. Not a thing in that silence indicates weakness. The men glance sideways, grin and nod. At last we know. The old beam will hold this much, though the deflection is nearly an inch.

But it is not yet the assigned weight.

He pumps again. The squeal begins anew. We listen and watch the deflection.

By then I am expecting the break, have told my small heart to prepare, have put my hand over my mouth so that if this old pine gives way, I will not scream any louder than this wood that holds my girlhood memory of riding the ropes these beams once held—and falling. That fall knocked the wind out of me for the first time and I thought I had died. Would the beam die?

But instead, it goes quiet as the final pounds are added. It doesn't break; it is as though it had to muster strength, gather its intentions. It holds just as anything that has held so much time and so many winters and even born its own destruction should hold. It holds the maximum number of tons for several minutes before Robert, satisfied, releases the pressure. My heart slows. We have the central beam for the kitchen.

Then they set up the next beam. This second one is worse—a serious crack in the final thousand pounds, deflection too great, and a shrill bawl at the breaking point. Robert says we shouldn't use it. It is a great crossbeam, and I remember balancing across that high beam, my brothers taunting me, the danger so great that I turned back. My only comfort is that it has not shattered. That means we might use it for a less demanding point load.

Their voices soften with strength.

The third one, oh that blessed third one, does not squeal, but calls out gently at the limit of the load—my father calling up from the lower barn that there is a new calf. That strength. We see then, standing among the men who know about wood and weight, how strong these beams can be, how lasting. No wonder that barn had stood a hundred years. The last ones we test are all solid, nearly quiet—soft-voiced as the night my friend and I slept in the hay, whispering secrets and vowing lifelong loyalty until dawn threw the shadows of the beams against the walls of hay.

The men from the yard nod, satisfied, and congratulate us before strolling away. They also hold a kind of pride about these old beams, a grudging appreciation. This is the work they do, the work with timber-framed structures. And this wood was once part of a structure they could build. Everything they believe about wood has been confirmed.

Sam reviews our house plans with David, exploring nonstructural ways to use the beams which have deflected too much. As they talk, I stand to the side—petting Blue—filled with a shimmering awe that fills up the hazy summer sky. Our beams will hold! After decades of being part of a working barn, after the pulling down and the winters covered with a tarp while waiting for our house to be ready for them, these great pieces of wood have not broken or rotted or become too old or unwilling to be what they are.

I have witnessed them come to the point of destruction for our own wills. But they have lasted, have held as memory and future hold themselves together. And they have given me their voices, their song of both work and weakness. I want these rough-shod things to hold up the house that will also hold the rest of our lives. I am filled with gratitude for the men who made the barn, for the old trees with their tight grain and their invisible strength. They gave their tree lives for shelter. And for the dream that will be fulfilled; we will reuse this rare resource.

All the way home, cold beers tucked illegally between our knees, we retell the stories of their voices, of how it felt to see them bend, of the quality of their pain-filled song of strength and weakness. We roll down the windows and let the wind take our dirty hair. The late afternoon is so bright, it makes our eyes water.

Window Pains

It's late fall, nearing December, and I am haunted by windows, by looking out, looking in, by the idea of the frame, the sashes, jams, rails and grids, words I never thought could be applied to something one sees through, to the invisible, and still the thing that frames the world one sees with every turn toward that opening. Windows are magic spaces, and we do not have them. That's right, not in the walls of the house that is now fully framed except for the most essential windows, the special-order windows, the big ones for the main floor.

Oh, we have the windows; they have been delivered, but they are not set in the frames, and the wind howls through the open spaces. As I address cards for the Solstice holiday, as I move through daily life in our rental house, I am nerved up about those unfilled spaces, gaps in the walls of our half-built home. We had done well, given that only three of us—Norm, David, and I—had worked on the house since early July. The walls were up, roof on, Tyvek stapled, doors in place. But where the largest windows should be, a crisis of emptiness. The house needed to be enclosed. The windows were there, placed carefully on flats, covered in tarps, huge with glass and dreams and distance I wanted to see every day I would live in it. These were our one indulgence in a house built on an artistic lifestyle and a tight-fisted budget, right alongside a commitment to both recycled materials and simplicity. But these huge windows had to be placed into those roughed out, empty openings, and sealed before the snow came, the winds blew, and most of all, before the dream could be ruined by leaving it open to the winter, that unpredictable monster of northern Michigan.

We had worked every weekend through the fall, but now a cold snap, and we knew: we couldn't work through the winter. Hell, we weren't even sure we could get to the place once the snow came. Now or never. But how?

We did what people in trouble do—we called our friends. With their help, we had finished other essentials of this unfinished nest: roof, soffits, fascia, the small windows and skylights. Now a final effort, an effort that would daunt us more than any other: we had to set only five windows, but they would not be easy. The three of these windows were two-and-a-half feet wide and ten feet tall. Ten feet. The remaining two were larger: five feet wide, ten feet tall, double-paned, six sections to each window. Without trusses or a crane, they had to be installed into openings six to eight feet off the ground on a thirty-degree, newly excavated slope. It was do-it-yourself suicide. But among people who build stuff, windows are a thing—it goes back to the magical; they are the embodiment of a house's eyes, a kind of seeing orifice; windows are the membrane between the interior and the exterior, between what happens in the nest and what happens outside of it, but is also the way that each side sees the other. We need windows; we love windows. Windows are the how light gets in, how it spills out at night. How the traveler is guided, how we know we're safe because we can see the monster a long way off. I wanted my windows big. I wanted them in place.

Five windows and a shaky set of borrowed scaffolding, two decent ladders, four friends: Steve, Jack, James, and Paul. Though we'd had plenty of help from women along our way, on this particular day, I was glad for their big-guy, upper-body strength. With David and me, that meant six of us.

First, we set the scaffolding up on the south side, bracing the legs on scrap lumber, leveling, leaving enough space between the scaffolding and house exterior to slide the windows in and lift them to the rough openings. Two men on the bottom, two men on side ladders, me and Paul on the scaffolding. Balancing the windows on two-by- fours, we lift in sequences, first to one pair of us, then the next. *Watch the glass. Watch the fingers. Watch your balance up there for heaven's sake.* Deep breath. Lift again. LIFT. My partner and I lift the window the last inch and shove. It bumps into place, and we hold it firmly with all our strength while the others scramble around us to level and square, then nail the frame. The wind comes up, chill and near freezing. I hear an old Queen song, maybe "We Will Rock You," drift from the radio David left on the oldies station, blaring in the room that will become the kitchen. I try to think warm.

Twice more we move scaffolding, reposition ladders, place and brace another window. Start lifting. Pull, pull, PULL UP. Set. Hold. Check level. Plumb. Square. Shims. Nail it. The three easy ones are done. We face the big ones, the beauties, the wonders that will call light into a house that would otherwise be dark. These windows face west where the sills are highest, where the slope falls away the fastest into the ravine, where there is no landscaping. It takes an hour to move and brace the scaffolding and set the ladders at their longest position. Someone grabs a back brace. Someone adds rope to the system. Gloves. Coffee. Think carefully. Is this the best way? Then, without a signal, we are moving into our places. Paul shouts directions. We muster strength and focus.

This window is larger, heavier, more cumbersome. The soil is soft and the scaffolding shudders with the weight. Through the grunting and the gruff barking commands to hold, *lift, lift, wait, pull,* this huge piece of light-filled glass rises. In a balancing act that would have impressed Ringling Brothers, we push it all the way to the top of the rough opening, and whoosh—slide it into place. Again, that final moment, nailing while balancing on scaffolding fifteen feet up. Everyone hangs on tight, everyone holds their breath. Then we breathe. One is in place.

The final one is the test. I try to assess time, energy, mood, and the utterly ridiculous fact of that scaffolding on another slope.

"Is this just too dangerous?" I ask. My back is aching for the first time in months.

David looks grim but shakes his head, "We have our friends. We're OK."

I won't say I was reassured; I won't say that I wasn't downright scared. I look over the ravine, over the leafless trees, the canopy of interlocking branches over our heads. I send out a call, will the land help us? Will our intentions be good enough? Silly, of course, this superstition that somehow the land would hear a plea such as this.

And in the process, there is shouting, scuffling, panting and groans, an almost-loss once, but then the next one rises like a sun, in and out of winter light. Is this possible? As we lift it, we wonder if it feels lighter than the others, something in the wood, or in our attitude at reaching this point. We do the work quickly. We do it.

After the last nail is in place, the wind stops at the glass that holds our reflections. We climb down and dismantle the ropes and scaffold. We step back into the house where, though it is still cold, the wind has died, and there is at last what I needed, stillness that promises protection. In the cold, the glass catches the last bit of afternoon sunlight before the long dark will come on, and the radio, turned low, blares on in its run of Queen hits, "We Are the Champions." We look at each other and chuckle, shaking our heads. How cheesy is that song? We have been nearly fools. But we have survived the windows.

I know it will be another year before we can celebrate the Solstice in this house, before I can honor the work of these red-faced, hearty folks with a toast and a meal. But as I join them, staring out through the windows of our new home, I imagine we are all looking through the dark for the future, for the sense of place and Being that seeing out and seeing in can bring.

Winter House

We took almost three years to build our home and still there are certain pieces of trim that are missing. Sometimes I whisper softly to David, "Baseboards" or "Crown molding." He's learned to ignore nuisance issues with an effectiveness that belies his dedication to making our home the best he is able to. But during that time when we were actually building, my real unrest sprang from the presence of winter. After the house was framed, during those winters we stopped working and sealed the construction site as best we could. We lived somewhere else. The last winter, I missed working on the house, missed the weight of my tool belt, the strength it took to raise a wall, to slide an appliance into place, to imagine the paint, then to paint those ten-foot walls. More than that, I felt an anxiety that, if it wouldn't actually lead to ulcers, offered some sleepless nights. I worried about snow weight, about rain blowing in through unsealed places before the siding was sealed, damp ruining the unstained floors, about pipes that weren't even run yet. I worried about windows that we had gotten in just before the first big snow—were they really secure? About light. Would there be enough light?

What a thing to think about.

One Sunday morning, I was so nerved up that David studied me over his coffee, then said, "Let's take a drive." We drove to the site. We burrowed the old Jeep as far up into Lake View Orchards unplowed roads as we could, then trekked in through snow to that beloved but unfinished house in the woods. And there, as we trudged down the slope, it stood pink with Tyvek in the small rough clearing, surrounded by empty trees and wind and winter stillness. David crowbarred the two-by-fours off the entry, pushed opened the knobless door, and we stepped into the space where we would someday remove our shoes.

In that unfinished house, I felt a muffled quiet so deep that it was like the walls themselves, framed and tangible. I felt the emptiness of unlivable rooms, the utter displacement of purpose in piles of flooring, tiles, and snaky tubing that would become radiant heat. I moved further into the uninsulated spaces, stood in an un-cupboarded kitchen, stepped before an invisible stove and sink. I thudded down into the lower living room, its high ceilings echoing in steely winter light. The woodstove, without chimney, sat like a hibernating bear in the corner, night-like and ominous. Everything felt like something it was not, could never be. Everything unfinished. I don't want to sound melodramatic, but that house was filled with such loneliness, it hurt to the core.

I wanted to fill it up, to seal the walls against cold and set the stove ablaze, fill the space with warm furniture, our favorite books, the family piano, the green pillows my mother had given us, plants, paintings, pottery. My dearest friends. I wanted to cry with the longing to make meaning in a space so fraught with—what was the word?—oh yes, abandonment. That's how I felt. I'd abandoned it. I leaned against the studs, fingering the crosspieces.

And then as I looked across the winter-chilled space, I felt the way silence can talk if you let it, how something empty can speak from its own unfinished being. The silence identified itself like church silence, or the silence one finds in great caves. It is a silence that turns larger if you let it, that stirs the imagination beyond the mundane expectations of interior decorating. It is not the silence of unrest or hostility, but the silence of acceptance that, if we are lucky, slides under unrest. It is the kind of peace one comes to when one lets what is unfinished, undone, unknown, be unfinished, undone, unknown. When one steps inside the cold.

I could not know when we would finish our home, or how soon I could ask my friends and family to join me in a joyful potluck, but I could be here, fully aware of the house in its aloneness. I could enter the moment, know that what we had so far completed would pull us like a strong rope toward the future. I could rest in this singular and forlorn hollowness, see it as hallowed, and embrace it.

I walked around the empty house, listening for a long time. I touched the cold glass, looked into every sawdusted corner, scuffed the floor which, despite some leaking, was not warped. We had done good work, and we needed to trust that. After I had listened in every room, I did what we all do with the spaces we love: I promised to be a good steward, to make this small house in the woods a place of fulfillment, which I understood now, I could only do because I also knew its loneliness.

In These Walls

When I was growing up in that hundred-year-old farm-house, my parents gutted a kitchen pantry to create an alcove for a refrigerator. When the dark wainscoting splintered off, they found a tattered packet of old letters and single-leafed bills that had fallen behind the molding and gathered dust in that gentle darkness. The letters were from the original owners of the house, an Irish family who, after fifty years of farming, gave it up shortly after World War II. Despite the fact that my mother dismissed the letters as ordinary, I found them mysterious and evocative. I read the unadorned prose and plain reports of births and marriages as messages deliberately tucked into the walls of the past to be deciphered in the present. I was sure I had discovered a great secret, that the letters had not fallen but had been hidden. I tried to tell my siblings that the common language in the letters was a code for declarations between lovers. My brothers snorted. I explained that the bills were another code which, once understood, would unlock the code for the letters. A code for a code, I claimed, relishing my cleverness. We had discovered a conspiracy to cover a scandalous secret from that earlier nineteenth-century family, something to do with a lost lover. Of course, in short order my mother put a stop to my imaginings. She would have none of it. She put a broom in my hand, work being her remedy for all wayward behavior and imaginings. But that one incident kept me happily pre-occupied with invented narratives rich enough to have delighted any romance editor or "True Confessions" publisher.

Eventually, those fantasies faded. What was left was the sense that something from the past was in the walls of our farmhouse, the idea that stories might, on occasion, seep out to touch us again. People leave things, lose things. Things fall in cracks, get left in the studs. During various farmhouse remodeling projects, coins, tools, and once a shoe surfaced from the innards of the walls. Though I no longer believed in the scandal, I came to recognize the subtler messages of a life having been held within in the walls of our home. If the past of a house can reach out and touch my imagination as it had, could the present of our house touch the future, be a catalyst for the imagination?

Three decades later, I am in the process of building my own home. I am no longer the immortal, invincible child. I am a woman who has earned her toolbelt, who has her own Estwing hammer, and who has come through melodrama to be as ordinary as my mother would hope. Well, not entirely.

I am conscious that my intrigue with those letters came from that quickening interest, the pleasure of discovering those other lives. I find myself thinking ahead. The house would outlive us; it was that well-built and unique. What would be left in these new walls when we had passed on? Would people find the amethyst earring I had lost while we were laying tile, or the work gloves that disappeared while we were running heat duct? And it came to me that one could leave messages, could deliberately attempt to make the future of this sturdy little house a message from the past. I stood in my house and imagined, at some far distant point, a wall being repaired, a room being expanded. What would they find? And then I knew.

Not a letter. Not a bill.

The electrical circuitry is tacked into place, the insulation is tucked between every stud. The drywall is stacked on the floor, ready to become the inner lining of the house. I have, during the spare, quiet evening hours, been reading and writing poems. Early one morning I rise, take a sheaf of poems I love best. I walk around the rooms of the house. Into what will be every wall of the house, I tack poems. Emily Dickinson and Walt Whitman. Auden and Yeats and Blake. Sara Teasdale's "Barter" and Elizabeth Bishop's "The Fish." Even some Beat poets. Tucked in with these great are my own rough drafts, perhaps the closest I will ever come to their ilk, my words tucked in the walls with Elizabeth Barret Browning and Robert Frost.

The workmen come. Though there is a raised eyebrow or two, they say nothing as they help put up the drywall and seal poems into our wall. Once mudded, you would never know the drywall hides a house full of poems. But sometimes, when we have potluck, certain tender people will ask, "You have rich conversation here, don't you?"

Or more directly "You like words, don't you?"

I'd like to believe it's not just that they know I'm a writer. And I wonder if it isn't working differently than I expected, not a message for the future daughter of the house, but the influence of words and images seeping through, slipping into the air, making the house whole with the spirit of poetry. The message in the walls is right now.

Stone Thanks

This was the Thanksgiving I had been waiting for—when I could finally host the feast in our new house. Everything on the first floor was complete; our dining room furniture was in place, our living room windows trimmed. We had a real kitchen with all the necessary accouterments. Everything on the first floor (the second was another story) was prepared except the bathroom tiling, the bathroom that our guests would use. For months we had stared at the gray Durock surface we had prepared, but as do-it-yourselfers, we had *hit the wall* on this one. We didn't have the know-how for the tile, the sunken tub and shower; we didn't understand how rocks, tile, and mortar worked. We had, however, discovered Scott Gordon, a tile artisan who didn't balk at the circular walls and the two-foot deep Roman-tile tub that had been the architectural nightmare in this house of dreams which we had, down to that bathroom, built mostly on our own. Now this wonderful craftsperson worked steadily for the third day, mortaring the four-by-four tumbled marble into place. To afford marble, we had purchased chipped seconds, and where the uneven, chipped corners came together, Scott cleverly set small, beautiful Lake Michigan stones that I had painstakingly collected during the previous summer. Every time we had gone to the beach, I combed the tumbling waves for unusual stones, then lugged them home like treasures for the bathroom project. He could paw through for the ones that matched the chips.

The day before Thanksgiving, as Scott neared the most difficult section of the job, I scheduled myself to the minute, preparing as much feast as possible ahead so I could enjoy my friends the next day. As I checked the two giant squash baking in the oven, poured pumpkin pies and simmered porcini rice, Scott appeared at the door of the kitchen.

"I'm running out of stones."

"What?" How was that possible? I had supplied two buckets brimming with stones. I had collected odd sea fossils, granite coins, quartz, the greens and browns I could not name, believing he would have more than enough for the entire job.

"The ones I have left are wrong." He led me to the bathroom where the stones, in all their beauty, filled the gaps between the tumbled marble. I loved the work he was doing, but I could see what he meant. The remaining stones either didn't match the missing corners or were the incorrect color altogether. He was nearly finished, and we had hoped the bathroom would be complete enough for visitors.

"I'll get more," I decided. "The beach isn't snow covered. I'll go right now and pick them. You keep working." I commanded, and he nodded and grinned. I turned off the squash, turned down the rice, set the pies to the side, and ran.

I didn't expect that cold November beauty, or the amazing fact that winter stones differ markedly from their more civilized summer siblings. I stood in gale wind and walked the beach, the bucket knocking my shins and sand burning my eyes. I knelt and chose, finally accepting that these stones would be darker, rougher, more reflective of the wild Lake Michigan I loved. An hour later, chilled but triumphant, I had filled the buckets with an entirely new kind of stone.

When I showed them to Scott, he nodded approvingly. He could see it too, could see the way this would texture the surface. But just as I was about to slide the squash back into the oven, he announced, "You'll have to bake them."

"Bake them?" What was he talking about?

"They have moisture in them. They've been in the rains and maybe waves since summer. The others were already dry, but not these. They need to dry. Fastest way is to bake them."

What about the squash and pies?

They would have to wait.

I poured the stones onto cookie sheets and cake tins and pizza pans, set the oven for four hundred degrees, and let the scent of water, weeds and fish overwhelm cinnamon and cloves. It was a strange hour full of wafts of summer, of light-filled dips and dead fish, of the scent of stones that hold spirits we do not imagine until they are forced out by the heat of an oven. An hour later, they were cooling like tarts on the porch. Scott surveyed the lot, then began selecting the ones that would make the bathroom into art.

As I bustled the pies back into the oven, I wondered, would pumpkin taste different baked in an oven that had heated stones? Would reheated squash hold the wet scent of a Petoskey stone's dreams? As Scott finished, I took a break and stood at the door of the bathroom. I could see the difference. Some parts of the floor and walls had a summer texture—flatter, gentle, lake-skimming stones. In others, Scott had left out whole tiles, and the squares filled with the stones clustered together, held a rougher, more unruly quality. It came to me, how like our lives, how we time ourselves to the rhythm of seasons, how we move in tandem with the surfaces of our shorelines and our winds and storms. I was thankful for the feast that would eventually be served, for the friends who would join us, for the skill of a fine craftsperson, but in that moment, I was most thankful for stones, dozens of stones from all our seasons, from July's warm balm to the November winds that make the wilder stones rise.

Autumn's Irony

Our house is as finished as a house built from adapted, adopted, adjusted materials and much revised plans—with me as one of the carpenters—ever will be. Instead, we turn to landscaping. The site, once lush with wild berries, is now abused with construction debris, and the surface is marred with backfill and infertile sand.

We eschew a lawn—unwilling to participate in a monoculture, water waste, the run-off, a power mower, and the social expectations. We opt for ground cover, and discover it is better all-round for the insects, birds, and the soil. We snicker about this: a lawn may have been a moot point since we had tucked the house so far into the dappled arms of forest, that even the heartiest domestic plants grew little but tendrils—it is that shady. There is so little summer light that chance of a lawn is nil unless we are willing to cut trees, and we have vowed—no more tree cutting. Thus, no lawn.

In the one or two spots that actually get light a few hours a day, we set beds of shade-tolerant perennials—hostas, astilbe, ferns—which will adapt. We invite the woods back in, coaxing leeks, Dutchman's Britches, Trillium, and wild columbine as close to the house as they will grow in disturbed soil. We plant myrtle on the south side, and let wild raspberry brambles reshape a northern jungle. They return with startling tenacity.

That summer feels as though something wild but cool will climb up from the leaf shadows, peer into our windows, or squeeze under the doors. There is a release from heat that wood-dark brings, even on the hottest days. This is what it means to become shade-tolerant, to embrace the trees. I am coming to love the way living in the woods encourages me to look at the shadows of the world.

In this time of climate change, we may need to embrace the forest more than ever. The Earth still relies on trees to rinse and renew the air. But as much as I appreciate that light-dapple falling on myrtle, and the vivid drama of autumn's wonder, that light and color foretells its own absence. I dread the winter palette, the loss of green and its familiars, the sunny blooms lighting what passes for our yard.

One September day at the post office in Empire, I find an abandoned Dutch bulb catalogue. The cover looks alive. I ask if I may have it, and Ginny the post mistress interrupts her letter filing to holler over the counter, "Oh sure. Folks just leave their extra catalogues. Help yourself." Then, glancing at what I am holding, she grins.

I pour over clusters of tulips, exotic daffodils, and those bravest hearts of all, the delicate-looking crocuses. I decide to order economy tulips and daffodils for naturalizing because as a first-time experimenter with perennials, I might make mistakes, and these seem forgiving. But how to choose? Only one way really. I pick for the pleasure of names: think of tulips named *Scarlet Dynasty, Queen of the Night, Lavender Rembrandts, Touched Greenlands*. A jonquil called the *Poet's Narcissus* makes me want to cry. That's not even mentioning the crocuses. The accumulative order for bulbs tops 400. We don't have money for this, and I don't care. There will have to be a flower payment plan.

Think of *Rose Angeliques*, and the payments hurt less.

They arrive in the brown UPS truck with instructions to keep them in the dark until the soil is cool, but I open every bag and roll the bulbs into my palms. Here is hope in its raw form, shaped like miniature turrets of exotic India. They promise to compensate for that now fast-approaching gray-brown-black-white palette of winter—the colors that ask you to stay put and keep quiet—insistent, demanding as a cat for the lap.

Think of *Autumn's Irony*.

Through that autumn, the bulbs bring me to my knees in late afternoon when soil is still warm enough to keep my hands from frostbite. The maples are still dropping their tarnished bits of sun like small prayers. The light grows immense, spilling now through an emptier canopy even as the Earth itself cools. Bless the Earth for at least trying to cool. I dig holes and press bulbs into soil, placing these plain but exotically named beings into the subterranean— essentially burying them. All through the process, planting clusters of daffs, lining up tulips and—where they will surprise me—dozens of crocuses, I am closing something alive off from an essential light that comes to my woods only with the autumnal equinox—after leaf fall. As the winter light blooms in the woods, the bulbs are as stilled as a name on a page before it is said out loud, dormant in a soft darkness. When I am done, no one but the dog knows where everything is planted, no one can tell what blooming anticipation is buried six scattered inches beneath the wide-open canopy. All is upside down with this season; it leaves me dizzy with wonder.

Just say *Touched Greenland.*

Moving into that forest winter, into its quiet and work, I dream almost daily of what will occur under the surface, that dark salvation in the lowest breath of color. I dream the longer hours of light that must melt the snow cover and warm the soil. I dream the temperatures will be timely despite a warming planet—not too early, not too late— and will soften the bulb in its own season, that the bulb will send out its worm-like roots, and that cream sphere will swell to bursting, the yellow-green spear splitting it open, pushing up with impossible insistence toward a new existence. I want the bulbs to shard our plain-as-mud yard with kaleidoscope contrasts to that earthy darkness. I want the trees above to slowly darken our woods again, as though we who live above the surface are slowly sliding under it. Blooming will be the hardest labor. I don't really know if it will happen at all. Sometimes it doesn't. Sometimes things green up but then wither. All I have is the promise of dirty knees, soil under my nails, the small burial in which I hope every upside-down heart rises, turning into a blossom like *Lazarus's Light*.

Left-Handed Imaginings

This fall, we are feeling the decade of work we've put into making a home. Making a handmade house means just that, doing much of it with our hands. We're feeling the pain in more than our scraped knuckles. And now, on top of that, a more practical drive. We need wood. For the woodstove. Lots of wood. Last winter had revealed our off-kilter calculation: multiple feet of snow and colder-than-expected temps. We burned through what we thought was a generous store of cords by March. We were forced to buy a couple cords to get through the final weeks, and that embarrassed us both—to be surrounded by trees and plenty of deadwood, and have to buy it?

The locals would have known better.

But this fact about our bodies: we are strong people, but the physical work has taken a toll. David can still split wood like a lumberjack, but his back is paying a price. And I have injured the ulnar nerve in my right elbow, and this means that for the first time, I cannot do my share of the labor, cannot easily lift, carry, or stack the logs. To compensate, we make a decision that pleases neither of us: for the first time ever, we will rent a gas-powered wood splitter.

He carefully backs this contraption that looks like an enormous insect onto the level spot where our woodpile once stood, on the edge of our woods. I leap out, full of energy, but as David explains the machine to me, I realize the only job of which I am capable is so simple that I won't even break a sweat. I am to stand on one side of the machine and with my left hand, control the steel wedge that splits the wood. I push it forward, and the blade moves forward into a log. It bites, presses that single sharp tooth into the grain. The log splits open, and the pieces fall to the sides. I pull the blade back. It slides back, releasing the log. Stops when I stop, rests when I rest. It would be miraculous for those of us who have spent days doing this work with maul and ax, but we miss the badass bravado of doing it ourselves. For the first time, I am not working myself into a fever of sore muscles, but instead stand quietly while David lifts the logs from the pile, places them on the splitter, catches the pieces as they are split, and tosses them into the truck bed. He works like a machine, this man. He will not be beaten by another winter.

I am so right-hand dominant that for a while, this simple task I am assigned demands all my concentration. It feels as though these left-armed muscles are unfamiliar with the logic and will of my head. Once, I push the lever the wrong way, and only David's quick withdrawal saves him from injury. I feel terrible, vowing not to make the mistake again. Instead, I focus on doing this small thing as well as I can. The repetitive work turns soothing, restful. Who would think that wood splitting with a rented splitter would have its own zen.

But standing there, doing this small work while David lifts and heaves, I think I ought to accomplish something. At least I can count, right? I decide to estimate how long this task will take—how long before we have enough to last an average, no—a serious, winter. I ask David how many halves or quarters we burn in a day. He guesses twelve, maybe sixteen if the temps turn bitter. If the wood-burning time of winter is one-hundred and fifty days or so, and we burn twelve or so pieces a day, we need roughly 1800-2000 pieces of wood. It should be easy to count logs as they are split, estimate how many pieces per hour, and announce when we have enough to keep us warm.

I stand in the wind, watching the logs, watching them drop neatly to the sides, counting, counting, but then I lose count, start over, lose count again. The sun addles me, the sound of the machine, a tenacious wandering of mind. How many times do I start over before I realize I cannot keep count? I try, but the variables of burning wood keep coming to me like small stories: wind—its direction and temperature around the old trunks and then the woodpile; moisture in the wood—how long has it been cut? What about the season's rain? The hillside where the tree trunks rested for a year—did it get sun or shade? The kind of wood: ash, maple, oak. The nature of the grain. How hot will it burn? How long will it hold embers? I think of the house as it weathers the weather, and again, I cannot count. I am lost in this motion, pulling the lever, this motion, thinking the small tales of these logs, every one which we touch multiple times: picking up, stacking, carrying to the stove, placing on the embers. All these lovely circumstances create the warmth of our home—not the numbers. The numbers are always off, not even approximate. These other things: seasons, weather, light and wind, even imagination, seem more reliable, though the results cannot be quantified.

So how do we ever know when we have enough to burn through a winter so long that it sometimes seems eternal? How do we know when to stop working, when our contract to warm ourselves as much as we can from our own acres, from the gifts of our woodlot, is fulfilled? I watch as the splitter works. There, each log opens itself to the wedge, the grain so straight that the log sometimes simply pops open even though the wedge has pierced only a few inches. Other times, the wedge hits a hidden knot and cobbles the piece, or the log screams and shreds as the long fibers let go of each other. Sometimes, the piece opens to a beautiful red core, sometimes there are dark lines like a current burned through one layer of the hypericum before the next layer came on. Sometimes the burls look like faces, or when the bark falls off, the smooth wood underneath is muscular. Nothing here can be counted, but it all counts, transposed into a warm living room during a dark blizzard.

Here and now, as I pull the lever, light comes up from the layer of dried leaves on the ground. My nose takes up with the half sweet, half earth scent of shorn maple. This is how it is, my left hand pushing and pulling while my right hand relaxes its dominance, stops counting, stops caring if or when there is enough for one hundred fifty days or not. We work for hours, this day made like a poem hovering over us, holding its numerics a secret, keeping its own left-handed joy.

Elegy for a Hardware Store

The poet, Nancy Willard, claims that hardware stores prove the existence of God. I believe it. For me, hardware stores have always been where the broken things of this world—the unfinished, undone dreams—were given hope. Hardware stores exist to offer humans the possibilities of gardens, fences, bird feeders, and whole houses where we could rest. They also gave me a vocabulary I loved for its quirkiness. How does one know a good life without having said *spanner flange*, rolling it around in the mouth until it becomes sexy? And what of the assonance of hardware: paints, pipes, plungers. In a hardware store, learning names was a treat for the mouth, and it made the future tangible; the world was a place that might work better because of what was found there.

So, can you blame me if I've met the closing of our local hardware store in Empire with grief? The store stood solidly, broadly, at the end of Main Street, its trim white clapboarding and wide porch like something from a Frank Capra movie set. It closed suddenly, with little notice. Its closing was the end of an era in my life. The Empire hardware store was my own personal hardware store. Or rather, it felt like it. When David and I returned to Leelanau County to build first a rough storage space for camping, later a garage, and finally the house, the hardware store saved our lives every day.

I was given my first tool belt—a tough canvas apron—as a freebie from that hardware store when we bought their entire stock of leftover roofing shingles at a deep discount. Several times a week, I refilled orders, learning the difference between galvanized and ARDOX nails, between treated and white wood. As our buildings progressed, David suggested I was ready for a heavier hammer, and it was at the hardware store where they let me try out an Estwing, its glimmering steel more beautiful than silver. I bought utility knives, tape measures, levels, and glue. Sue, the woman who worked the counter, automatically handed over new carpenter's pencils because I constantly lost mine. She showed me how to reload the roof stapler and the caulking gun. When David and I shingled the garage, the hardware folks sold us a weathervane on deep discount because they were having as much fun as we were. They wanted things to work, to operate properly too. And always there was lumber, a small but effective yard that kept us going through miscounts, mismeasures, and miscuts. They let us sort through the two-by-fours and cut rebar to length when we were landscaping a terrace. It was from that hardware store that David purchased my second tool belt, powder blue leather, now gone gray with dirt and wear. He bought it as both a warning and honor badge just before we started to shingle the house with white cedar that we'd driven deep into the Upper Peninsula to purchase from a ninety-year-old miller who had only three fingers on each hand. I couldn't have been prouder.

By then, that hardware store was stamped on my soul. I could walk into the garden section and pick up a trowel that fit my hand. I knew where they stored oddly sized screen doors, crown trim, a small but essential display of fishing lures, greeting cards, and mousetraps. They ordered the birdseed my birds liked (or so I believed), and they had the special glue we needed for the subfloor. We could even pull our township permits there in the hardware store, sketching dimensions at the counter while Sue and Leo rang up anchor bolts and sill seal.

More than anything, I wished I could have said goodbye to my hardware store, could have walked through the aisles under that too-bright fluorescence, lingered in front of the dozens of boxes of nails, run my hands over the rows of caulking, and dived once again into a bin of copper fittings. I wanted to traipse out with a dozen bags of compost or treated four-by-fours, emergency candles, flashlight batteries, hoses, hooks, tape—all on a close-out sale. I wanted to offer farewells to the kind people who watched me learn to say the word *bitchathane* (slang for *bituthene*) without blushing.

I stand before the empty store at the end of Main Street in Empire. Our house is as finished as it will ever be—a house is never done. I know that now, and that makes the closing especially hard. That hardware store had stayed open and was vitally important through three different ownerships before finally being lost to the greed and vagaries of a big company and competitors. A big corporation whose name would be familiar to most anyone bought it in order to close it, to destroy the competition.

Where am I going to rediscover that the world, though not perfect, is not mad either? Where but in a hardware store will I be able to trust that my universe is a place to be sorted and ordered, a place where repair is possible, a place to be given the forecast of hope and the stuff to make it happen?

The Path

Late in the cooler evening, I walk from my Think House, the one-room shed that now serves as my writing studio and den. I open the door to our house, entering from the chill, to find my husband brushing yet another coat of oil on the new cabinet that he is building from a black cherry tree that blew down in a windstorm four years ago. This is something we have tried to do—give purpose to natural things that come our way, even fallen trees.

David loves to work with wood and has made our house trim boards, base boards, and cabinetry from found or given materials. Watching him split logs from wood cut on our property, or recut old boards scarfed from a barn for the picnic table, I feel the old passion rise. He likes to use recycled wood not only because it's generally cheaper, but because it has history, character, and is sometimes of better quality than new wood. I love best our redwood and fir grill table made of recycled scraps saved from an old deck he once took apart for a friend. I especially like watching him work with the planer, the machine that makes the wood come clean of its roughness. With its shrill whine, this machine smooths the wood surface by peeling the slimmest layer off the rough boards. The by-product is the fine wood curls that sliver off the planer. These ringlets, in their own way, are as lovely as the new and shining boards. The thin shavings are like curled pages, miniature scrolls that hold messages of work and pride. I sift through coils of pine, ash, and cherry so fine that if I unroll them, they break in my hands. Whenever I enter the garage, the sweet-sharp scent of the shavings pile mounded under the planer, tells me all I need to know about my husband's creativity. Now he's making a border of walnut for the cabinet, now a small pine table for the cabin, now a stool for a five-year-old to sit on.

But what to do with those shavings? For a while, these were dumped unceremoniously onto the compost pile until we discovered they didn't compost as fast as vegetable matter and caused a slow-down in the composting. For a long time, we found no way to reuse this dry mash of curling beauty and light, and he would simply scatter them back into the woods.

In late winter, after supper and dishes, I often walk back out into the dark to the Think House to write for as long as my mind will focus. This is the small building we also built by hand to house my writing, set east of the house, a one-room space of rustic simplicity where I write and yes, think. At this time of year, it always seems like a long, dark walk because we do not have streetlights on our road, not even a yard light, and the interior lights on this side of the house are turned off after we clean up from supper. I have learned to watch for one tree silhouette, a bit darker than the other darks, on the edge of the driveway and to step left of it, moving on a diagonal through the trees. Sometimes the path is so dark that I feel my way forward through my feet, using the harder texture of the path to guide me. With more than a little of that old childhood fear of the dark rising in my throat, I search the night for the edge of the deck, for the step up into the cabin. More than once I have bumped into a dark corner or misjudged distance, and found myself well into the woods before some faint shape offered back my placement in the world. Once, coming back from the Think House, and watching only the light of the house, I tripped off the deck steps and landed in the wood pile, alarming several nests of mice. With a thoughtful look, David touched my scraped shins.

The next evening after supper, I close the door of our kitchen to traipse out to the Think House. The new moon offers only the slim light that wild animals feel safe in. I search for the tree that will place me on the path. And there the path is, to the left of the tree. I can see it. I can see the path during a new moon? A soft, just-visible glow, a pale way on the floor of the dark woods. Understanding arrives in a rush. I step forward, secure now, onto a thick rug of light-curled shavings leading all the way to the step up and into the room where I unfold my own unwritten pages with gratitude and acceptance for the gift of wood and love.

Millennium

*Y2K bug, also called Year 2000 bug or Millennium Bug, a prob-
lem in the coding of computerized systems that was projected to
create havoc with computers and networks around the world
at the beginning of the year 2000 (in metric measurements k
stands for 1,000). After more than a year of international alarm,
feverish preparations, and programming corrections, few major
failures occurred in the transition from December 31, 1999, to
January 1, 2000.*

> *—Encyclopedia Britannica*

We are now so well-ensconced in the twenty-first that the
turning of the twentieth seems ancient history. Old hat certainly. Most young people reading this won't even remember
the hoopla. But 1999 had been a crisis year, not because of
flu or politics, but because of computers. The Y2K bug, as it
was called, had sent IT departments scrambling, and in the
midst of the head-scratching about how to solve the calendar
problem, the doomsayers and dooms-dayers prepared us to
watch the end of the world as we knew it.

The problem was simple. When the computer age began,
no one thought about the turn of the millennium. I'm over-
simplifying here, but it was a calendar issue, and looked
like the turnover from one millennium to another would
compromise all data, the inner workings of everything held

in memory from recipes to banks. Anything in a computer system that used a calendar could collapse—would collapse—if we didn't take action. By Solstice of 1999, some small assurance that it could be solved was being floated. But only the die-hard techies were sure. Pundits wanted to garner more reaction out of scare tactics, so media-instilled anxiety remained high. TV anchors forecasted doom. How do you celebrate this New Year among a thousand New Years, and make it stick when the apocalypse might arrive the next day—or so the fear-mongers would have us believe? Most people double stocked pantries, just in case.

So for most of us, the evening came with quiet worry. What to do until midnight when we would learn if those IT wizards had done their work properly? We had trust in those guys, but we were Janus about it, looking both ways. David and I had actually, laughingly, stocked the basement pantry with batteries, extra water, basic dry goods, cans of our favorite spaghetti sauce, and lots of TP. Not enough to last long, but enough to claim, if things went south, that we had prepared. And there were enough power outages in our remote area that it wouldn't go to waste.

Also, we felt alone. We were four years into our new house, and we still hadn't managed to make inroads into Empire's village life—they were nice but always cautious. We were not local. They didn't include us. If there was village stuff going on, it was kept among themselves, and a mix of Y2K worry and basic isolationism had quelled even this momentous New Year.

Outsiders ignorantly call Empire sleepy. Not true. The bowling tournament down main street in the middle of winter, the four-stand farmer's market where the best black-market unpasteurized cheese and honey are sold "under the table," the infamous polar swim—a rite of passage I could not manage—all marked the village as vitally awake. Still, it's an insular place, run by people who just might deliberately keep their village invisible as Brigadoon. That kind of blinkeredness is hard to break.

So I don't believe the news I hear first in the grocery store, the wonder-laden word—"Fireworks."

"Fireworks?" I ask, incredulous. The township had banned them for decades.

"Tonight. On the beach." Whispers. Sidelong glances. Nods.

"When?"

He names a time. Yes, deep dark by then. But was this a joke?

"Who's doing it?"

"Hmmm. Ummmm. A private citizen."

"Fireworks?" Were they pulling my leg? But for this New Years, after this crisis, well yes, fireworks would be right. Defiance even more so.

"Be there."

I walk out with wine and on-special red peppers, along with a dream that the New Millennium might be marked with something other than a Y2K nightmare. The wind coming down the street pierces my jacket, and I wonder if I have heard this right. To reinforce my doubt, when I tell David that there will be fireworks on the beach that night, he laughs aloud, *Naaah*, shakes his head and wanders back to his football game.

I check the Y2K closet. Along with the Y2K stock and the usual weird stuff that pantries gather—green pepper pesto, anchovy paste, canned fruit juice—I'm looking for the sparklers from the last fourth of July. I find half a package.

I suspect this whole thing is a bust, but I like the idea of something light-hearted in the midst of all this "technology will bring us down" hoopla.

That afternoon, I realize that I have forgotten a bottle of champagne for what we suspect will be the quietest New Year ever. Thinking that at least we can pretend, I drive back to Empire grocery store just at closing. I ask the owner, a friendly man whom I admire for good sense and quick wit, "Are there really going to be fireworks on the village beach tonight?" If this is some kind of scam, he will tell me.

"*Shhhhh*." Like this was top secret, he ducks his head, looks around, waves me behind the deli counter. He looks hard at me as though assessing whether or not he can trust me. "Yeah. There'll be fireworks." Then he grins and darts away to cut a ham the size of a small tank.

Back home, I tell David, "We've been invited. It's a sign they like us."

He looks skeptical.

That night, dressed in heavy jackets, we pull into the village beach. No one is there. Not a car, not a body, not even a stray gull. We don't look at each other as we sit quietly for a full five minutes. Then he says, "Look. Don't feel bad. To them, we're still new in town. Don't blame them if they want to take you for a ride. We're not locals yet." He's trying to be diplomatic.

"We've been here four years, dammit." So much for diplomacy. "We are NOT newcomers. We've spent a lot of hard-earned money in this village." But I know. Money means nothing compared to time and bloodlines. Still, I can't help feeling betrayed.

"Well," he looks around the wide, empty beach, and sighs. "It doesn't look promising." But he's seen the look on my face, and he knows when to be quiet.

Three minutes of silence later a car pulls in next to us. Then a pickup.

"See?" I say.

"So there are other suckers."

I gasp; he apologizes promptly.

But in the next several minutes, dozens of vehicles swoop into the parking lot. Finally, a rusty pickup backs out onto the access ramp where the old boats launch. By that time, most people's headlights are splayed over the windy, snowless beach, highlighting sleeves of foaming white caps. A small boy in a red jacket darts across the sand. Another child in a green parka rockets into the light, swinging her arms and looping in the wind. Suddenly there are children flittering like bats over the sand, and then adults bundled thickly as upright bears moving among the bright shadows. The truck, backed down the ramp, is surrounded by dark-hooded men who, from a distance, look like ancients in monk tunics, throwbacks to yet another millennium.

From the back of the pickup, they pull a large bundle. Despite the uneven beams of the headlights, we identify a bale of recycled cardboard bound by metal strips. The men lug it down the ramp. Another man shadow-steps forward and begins spraying, casting the spell of gasoline onto the folded Delmonte, Nabisco, and Spartan boxes. Someone tosses a match, and the huge cube springs up into a bonfire, marking the shoreline for miles. The flames woof in the wind, and it is then, in the light of this sooty chemical magic, that we see the beach highlighted with villagers, whole families made both substantial and ghostly by the flickering blaze. Some dance, some gather around the smoky pyre, some stand alone, backs to the wind, sentinel.

I would have been content with this display of village funk, but then several men carry a wooden door covered with what appears to be upright metal coffee cans. They set it down beyond the bonfire, farther down the ramp, almost to the water's edge. Someone slips out of shadows and lends a Zippo flame to a slim fuse. Someone steps back and shouts *Stay back*. There is the kind of tension that only happens when you feel like a child, whether you are one or not. And then the piercing whistle, the streaming trail up, up, up into the millennial sky. Whoosh! A huge zinnia flays that dark curtain, swept sideways by wind.

David powers up the radio, broadcasting celebrations from the Irish sessions at New Grange to New Zealand aboriginal drummers. As the next pyrotechnic display shoots skyward, horns blare and kids cheer.

We abandon the truck, join the villagers to blow kazoos, whistle, hoot, stamp our feet. I pass the sparklers to the children, and they draw swirls and arcs against the darkness. With each bright flower pluming over Lake Michigan's winter night, we celebrate the new age, whatever it may bring. It clearly won't be easy. But when I look around, a man wearing a frayed army jacket pulls a silver flask from his coat. He catches me looking and raises it to me before tipping it back. I grin at him, at David, and we join in singing happy birthday to the millennium, to this communal act of defiance. One after another, with each vivid explosion, the village repels the apocalypse.

Sweet Cider

Listen. How it is done is important. First, you must pick windfall apples from a local orchard: buying them without spending an hour in the orchard of their source reduces the sweetness. You must believe this. If you don't pick them yourself, you won't have seen the land, the orchard sloping toward the sunset, or felt the way the air wafts with a floral scent gone to silk rags. You won't have talked with a stranger about the year this orchard was planted by old man McClary, decades ago, and while many trees have been replaced since that original planting, there are heirlooms among the newbies: Wolf River, Snow, Wealthy, Grimes, and the nearly ancient russets. When you have touched the Earth and its fruit just enough that it feels like home, you must bring a wild selection of these apples to the bed of the truck and pour them into the galvanized tub that came to you from the family's centennial farm. You must fill the tub with water from the 200-foot-deep well and wash them as though each was a story. Each is.

Then you must set up the press. Screw the wooden basket the size of a bushel to the top chute, then line the slatted barrels with nylon filters, and set the barrels below the chutes and the basket. Toss the first handful into the basket, but don't fill it quite up—you want to feel how it works first. Grab the crank and turn. It will surprise you how they

resist at first. It is as though the apples must learn they are
made of sweet water, of rain, pith laced with apples' peculiar nectar. They thought they were firm—they had stood
against the storms. But the press does the work. Like many
old machines, it was made for mechanical beauty, a technology that lacks all things microchip, but holds the visible
logic of objects for which obsolescence is impossible. The
press makes a plain sense, holds an aesthetic of its own. Its
structure springs not merely from a need to survive, but to
make something rich and sustaining.

Turn that crank. Not only is it harder, but noisier than
you thought, a happy chokity-chokity as the gears of the
press break the apples into coarse mash. Like anything that
must be transformed, first this breaking down. Fruit or walls
or bigotry or simply mistaken expectations. As if winter is
not hard. Turn that handle until the barrel below the basket
is spilling over with this sluice of something sweet that
you will make from something broken. We do this with
apples, sometimes with pears, with the arts and even with
our hearts. We do this with friends who gather, bringing
other wild apples and their own jugs. Sometimes we do this
with history, though that gets dicey depending upon your
point of view.

Slide the barrel forward so the rim is directly under the
press. Now put your strong hands on the wheel which has
been still and silent next to the basket. Turn the wheel. The
press, that layered circular thickness slowly lowers itself,
an implacable flatness that fits exactly into the rim of that
barrel. Turn the wheel and crank the press slowly down the
grooves, lower and lower into the barrel that is filled with the
mash. The barrel has no bottom, just the net, and this makes
it possible to compress the mash. As the mash is tamped

further into the barrel, the juice spills out the bottom, down another chute, and the cool golden liquid spills out into the steel bowl, at first in a slow run, then gushing. Keep cranking. Again, it is work to bring down the press, just as it is work to change anything. Watch as the dripping becomes a lush rush, juice spilling off the chute, splashing apple nectar into the deep bowl, filling it with the unpasteurized fruit brew.

Taste it twice. Taste it right now, before chemistry takes over. This will be the simplest and purest of its flavors, that first press, sweet and complicated as first love, first dances, first picnics, first time you leapt from a high swing. Then strain and rinse the netting, and maybe do some other work for the time it takes to press another bushel. Then taste that first juice again. It will already be browning. Here is the trick apples play with air. The juice is oxidizing, and if you taste it now, you will feel the tingle of transformation, feel the poems you know by heart, the names of old quilts, a shirt fresh from laundry, the weather of the season in which you were first kissed, and perhaps the hands of people who planted the tree. Well, perhaps not all of that, but what happens is that the flavor enriches, grows deeper, like aging, like living. Unlike the artificial clarity of store-bought, super-filtered apple juice, fresh sweet cider transforms to this uncelebratory sweet brown.

Strain each new barrel through layers of cheesecloth to filter those small chunks of mash or leaves or renegade seeds that hold traces of cyanide, and see how every drop singes itself in the frost-laden air, as though its color prophesies the dying of the gardens. But the sweetness, the sweetness as you stand in the light of good work is reward for harvest and also a pledge—winter nights will be less dark, warmed by cider, by this human intersection with trees, easing past

145

the burden of labor. Finally, the most important part, the final step of this November work. Carry jugs of filtered cider into the house, pour it off into the pot, heat it up with cinnamon and nutmeg, then pour it slowly into chipped cups. For some, you may need to cut such an abundance with the gasp of brown liquor.

Believe that this simple making is more than good work; it is yet another link to each other, a metaphor for our interconnection with land, each other, our abilities as makers and lovers of the planet. And when the pressing is done, take the mash that has been scraped into the wheelbarrow and feed it to the pig, or dump it in the high meadow to feed the deer and the creatures who sift quietly through the dark. They too, in this intersection, must be honored.

Part III

Kuieren

Zullen we gaan kuieren?

("Shall we go for a stroll?")

Dutch Verb—*kuier; kuiert; kuierde; kuierden; gekuierd*
To amble, stroll, saunter, walk, or wander

The Understory

They call it *the peak*. I suppose you could apply it to life in our forties too, but as I mean it here, we are talking trees. The peak is not some period of sexual prowess anticipated by every young man and woman who hit their stride, but instead the tree population of the entire state. Of course, one can discover sensory titillation in being a tree-peeper: there are competing reports for the best hot-colored trees, for bright images snapped with expensive cameras, even for the cheapest hotel room on the boundary of the Manistee National Forest where the viewing is best. The peak is a time so fraught with the quest for color that buses full of delighted blue-hairs seek the "peak" as it billows across the Peninsulas, searching for the height of color as it shifts through the various counties. Even here along the lake, our weather anchors attempt to predict the peak, usually around October tenth, that day when sugar maples and poplar will be at their most brilliant reds and yellows. And we refuse to admit the classic reproach from the old timers who, when asked what day the leaves will be at their peak, chuckle and say, "No such thing. Wind blows 'em off before they peak." In fact, our peninsula winds, rising in intensity and duration at that time of year, often do pull off the leaves, leaving trees empty-handed, and all those phone cameras in a state of disappointed reproach.

But here is the secret. When the peak is at its best for those big views from the scenic turnouts, for those high elevation afternoons at Picnic Mountain, the show has not even begun in the interior of the woodlots. Inside the woods, it is still green. One has to wait then; there is yet another revelation. Days or weeks after the natural drop, or after the flurried wind pulls down the leaves and opens the canopy, the most golden time of autumn begins. When the unmasked sky is revealed in the lace of empty trees, when nights with frost have become more common than those without, and when I am often busy carrying out the ritual of the "lasts," the understory arrives. And only with the turning of the understory, the coloring of the smaller trees: birch, beech, and baby maples, do I feel the awe everyone else seems to feel about the peak.

Maybe I am putting the summer garden to bed, bringing in the last of the tomatoes, having left the green ones as long as possible. Or I am raking leaves, and the piles are whispering their vibratory words. Or I am gathering the small garden tools from where I have left them in trenches and furrows. I am turning the compost pile or picking the last round of apples for the cider press. I am dressed in my old blue plaid work jacket. I am bending to the task under the wide mouth of the October canopy. I lift the fork, the rake. I drop the apple into its wooden bushel and see—not above me in the high trees, nor below me in the ravines, but at eye level—in a blaze of light that has not infiltrated this place for half a year—the thicker gold of the understory.

Or maybe I just wake to it—that story under the stories of canopy and heights. It almost always takes me by surprise. It is, yes, like waking.

It is all around me then, that other story revealed under the higher stories of the tall trees. The ground covered with yellow, the light reflected more from Earth than from sky, light coming from the solid dirt at my feet, surrounding my old work boots, and all the small curly-headed, thicket-bound scrub maple and shrub birch are showing off like children, *look at me, look at me.* Here is the closer story, what is really happening in the woods—the hidden revealed.

How it goes: first, there is relief. Everyone has left the big show. No one is here. Then the rake drops from my hand, and I walk away from the yard, off the path, stepping onto the light that is layered, shining upward, not falling, and is almost palpable. The land is glowing, incandescent. I don't reach up, but stretch my arms horizontally, breathing the trees' breath in living color. It comes to me: I am growing older. The work will be done soon. It is not a sorrowful knowing; it is the truth inside the understory.

Or perhaps it is a day when David and I are putting up wood together. Perhaps we stop, pass hot cider from the old thermos, hand to hand, stand and stare at the plot unfolding before us, one that is not a step-by-step loss, but in the blaze of color so close—this is what we do to love each other now: we embrace the understory, the golden, lovely way that is closer to Earth, the light coming up from the ground, the secret story that has no words but is golden.

When that happens, I want to shout. *Here is the real story.* Here is the *un-peak*, the way we will find our way to the sky.

Early Snow

I was teaching research in the library at Traverse City's Northwestern Michigan College when it began. I hadn't seen good lake-effect snow in a long time, not in the five years I had been away, living in a big city. In fact, though Chicago winters could be remarkably cold, and it certainly snowed, their snow wasn't like our snow here in the Michigan I had returned to, the Michigan of my childhood. For one thing, it was rarely this kind of lake-effect—big puffy flakes coming down in the gentlest of falls.

This snow launched itself before noon, and by the time my one o'clock Comp class was underway, with students going from stack to stack in the library, I could barely take my eyes from it. But I had to teach.

The students' research assignment was to discover a new vocabulary, a technical or mechanical manual that offered a vocabulary with which they were unfamiliar, but that they could use to create metaphor. They were to write an essay that extended that technical language toward a new meaning. Most of the students had now chosen their manuals, everything from plumbing to bread baking, and were settling at the tables near the front desk of the library. But they were not happy. They were learning that it's hard to make metaphor. I was learning that it's hard to teach it.

I should have been circulating among them, but I was distracted. The snow, this snow. I wanted to sit in front of those tall library windows and watch the snow falling among the great white pines. I caught myself turning to the librarians at the desk, asking them, "Isn't it incredible? Isn't it beautiful?" They sighed. Some students, overhearing, snickered. Some looked alarmed—they will have to drive home on unplowed roads. For them, snow that came this hard, this early, was not welcome.

First snow is as hard as metaphor.

Still, the young librarian with the brown eyes at the main desk smiled at my enthusiasm. She made an effort, "I suppose there should be a word for this first snow."

"You don't like it," I asked.

"No more flowers for a long time."

Her answer seemed thoughtful. I marveled again at something I had noticed since my return to Michigan's Grand Traverse. People here seemed, if not kinder, at least more sensitive. Maybe it was me; maybe I was happier, and that helped people respond. But another part of me felt that the big city, for all its excitement, energy and opportunity, didn't always induce the best in people. I had become hardened to brisk attitudes and hurried responses, not this careful answer—a word for the first snow, a remark about flowers.

I returned to the kids at the tables, hooded jackets and stocking caps shoved aside, trying to assist with vocabularies that were surprising and sometimes unpronounceable. It seemed they understood, but were not invested, or at least not fully. Some were enjoying the words, the innovations of language, but there wasn't a lot of enthusiasm—that snow had their attention as well. How could they care about new metaphors? The snow was becoming the hardest part of the assignment.

How could I blame them? Even as I moved between tables, I glanced at the squall, deliberately passing in front of the big windows as often as possible. The ground was fully covered now; a few playful snowballs were being lobbed among the trees. I pulled back, made myself pay attention to my students. That was why, when the older man burst through the front doors of the library, I didn't at first notice.

A student had asked a question about the language of smelting iron. I answered. Then, as I moved to another table, I heard his voice, spoken in the low insistence that captures attention. I looked across the tables to the library counters. This older man leaned in at the circulation station. He was dressed in tattered clothing barely warm enough for this weather. He wore a colorful baseball cap; his hands were covered in gray mittens with frayed fingers. His voice was raspy, anxious. Something had upset him.

"I don't know what else to do," he said.

Students, with that sixth sense for a scene, looked up from their manuals. No different from them, I eased closer.

The brown-eyed librarian faced him, his body shielding an object. I could see her face, but not what rested between them.

"Where did you find them?" she asked.

"In the woods. Someone just threw them there."

The young woman spoke softly, "Maybe you should take them back."

His body shifted, and as he stepped nervously aside, I saw what they were discussing—a huge bouquet of two dozen red roses, set in presentation style, dotted with snow. "But they'll freeze," the man burst out. "I saw them early today, when I was picking up cans. I didn't know what to do so I watched them. Nobody come, so I brought them here. But I don't know. I don't know." He moved his cap forward, then back, staring at the roses.

I could see why. These were not ordinary roses; these were not the one-dozen-for-cheap you can get at the grocery for Valentine's Day; these were those long-stemmed, special-order-ahead from a florist—and two dozen! Two dozen deep red wonders, open only enough that you could see how big the bloom would be when they opened fully, so thick-stemmed and fresh, they didn't need wire to hold the blossoms upright. Their lushness matched the satin bow, and the baby's breath and soft green fern, a little tattered now and dotted with clumps of snow, framed the elegant arrangement. The roses were held inside stiff cellophane that caught and reflected light—though this wouldn't have protected them for long from the cold.

My students, glancing sideways, watched the scene unfold, as attentive as they had been all day. What I knew, what we all knew: this had been a deliberately planned and ordered bouquet. Drake, the student sitting nearest me, the one who had selected a manual on plumbing, murmured, "Wow, those cost a bunch." Right on, Drake.

The brown-eyed librarian studied them in awe. She was silent for so long that the man seemed overcome with agitation. "I just don't want them to get ruined. They'll freeze out there in the woods. No one will find them if they get covered with snow. No one will enjoy them." He knew their value, knew that you don't leave roses in the snow, knew the winter would come without flowers. He picked at the cellophane. The sound, a small crackling, seemed to wake the woman from reverie.

"There was no card?" she asked.

155

"No. I looked."

"You didn't see a florist's label?" She parted the torn cellophane and looked among the stems. He was right. There was nothing to tell her who they were for or from.

"Seems like they should be for someone," he was nodding his head up and down. And then he looked at her, "Seems like something musta happened. No one just drops flowers into the woods. It's bad. Dontcha think?"

I could see her weighing the situation. I could see her wondering about the man. I could see the story open in her mind as it was opening in mine, as it was opening in the minds of all my dear students who watched from their tables, some idly, some with the same intense interest. Who would leave two dozen high-quality, high-dollar roses in the woods on the day of the first snow? And why? Had there been a fight? Were they a rejected apology? Were they a come-on that had failed? And if so, what act would have caused a hurt so great that one would toss such flowers into the snow? And what if this man had something to do with the story? I turned to my class, thinking to direct us back to our work, but they were all watching. It came to me: these flowers held not just beauty but the allure of narrative. We all felt it: the longing of the man, of the flowers even. The drive of story. And this was the beginning of what promised to be a long winter.

We wanted the warmth of narrative, its long-stemmed, thorny beauty.

Finally, the librarian spoke. "Why don't we keep them here on the desk? Then everyone can see them. And you never know, maybe the person who put them in the woods will claim them. We can take care of them for you."

The man's face turned less weary, and he nodded. "That would be OK." Then he nodded again, pivoted, and walked out the door, waving his gray-mittened hand without looking back.

The brown-eyed woman found a chipped vase, filled it, set the roses in, and there they towered over the counter and the books, holding their secrets. As she was rearranging the stems, the students drifted back to their manuals, though a few spoke softly about the scarlet flowers, about the small incident they had been privy to, as though they had accidentally looked inside a private moment. As I returned to them, Drake, chewing on his ponytail, shook his head and sighed, "Whatever this is all about, it's gotta be sad."

Then Clare, next to him and the quietest of them all, asked, "Are there manuals about roses?"

Were we all making up the tales in our minds? The Clares and the Drakes? I wondered if the stories they made would tell us about those roses, or would they rather tell us about who we were, what sorrows we were made of. And what of roses, those flowers both beautiful and cliched, full of literary history gone stale, a hundred poetic allusions that had been also lost, the many novels and commercials, lordy, all the commercials? Yet roses survived, both wild and domestic, into the cultural traditions and gestures of human celebration: declarations and apologies, birthdays and anniversaries and funerals. Weddings. And what of these particular hot house creatures? These were cut in the hothouses of Ecuador or Columbia, made their way through the cold chain of refrigerated travel, and by the looks of them, had made it in time to assure the twelve days of their "fresh" look. Except for a few darkening petals, these had managed to come the whole way—until the snow. These were holding now, not as flowers, but as the not-yet-fully-open blooms for story, the beginnings of some narrative of loss.

Metaphor is not yet story, but brings depth to stories that will yet be made. What do those roses represent? It was all that my students needed. Yes, Clare, there were manuals on roses. All this is suddenly in my mind, and in the minds of Drake and Clare and others, each in their own way, making the tale more explicit. The snow, the roses in a chipped vase, the man—all were seeds of meaning to be picked up and nurtured, a story left in the woods until we find it, the rough lines of narrative our lives and minds gave us. Roses in the snow, a beginning, a step forward toward the winter, and finally, a metaphor to be shaped from the language of flowers.

Weather Changes

On an early December day filled with the kind of snow that invited one to play, I drove to Mason County, to the house on the river where my parents have retired. All the way, white tulle floated down in the same way that a good dream moves—slow and content. Nothing looked cold, and I felt joyful as I swung the pickup through backroads. Part of my mood was the anticipation of seeing my parents, especially my father, buoyed by their good news. My father, after a serious surgery and six months of chemotherapy, was officially in remission. His doctor was so confident that he had removed the port through which chemo is administered. My father, a cheerful octogenarian who still drives to the family farm nearly every day, was his old self, and I was thrilled to join him in our annual ritual—cutting the holiday tree.

Once there, my father took over, spinning the truck through back fields to the pine plantation which draped the farm's boundaries like a great snake. My brothers had long ago made the decision to plant trees only on land that could not otherwise be tilled. That decision created an adventure for us as we weaved around steep slopes and over surprise bluffs. Deeper and deeper into the untilled land we drove, finally into wilder, untrimmed trees, where certain trees might not ever be cut—some deformity—hole in the side, trunk curved as a scythe or doubled as the victory sign. These were the trees I loved. I wanted holes—places to put the stuffed animals or to dangle the heavy glass ornament from Holland. I wanted the wilder trees, trees that, like wilder folks, have hidden potential.

We found it on the east hillside, a tree with a dense shape, but lopsided in the back—it would face the corner and not take up space in our small living room. I was delighted with its eleven-foot height and funky branching. As I thanked the tree for its life, snow continued with the year's quiet end.

Dad huffed, carrying his sturdy crosscut saw up the slope. We cleared snow from low branches, and he knelt under it, his torso disappearing into green. He sawed away, his body moving with the thrust and pull of the crosscut, but after only a few minutes, he pulled out. "Lean against the trunk; that will open the cut and make it easier for me." I leaned. He went at it more slowly, the teethy crosscut finally sounding like an engine winding down. It stopped, but the tree did not fall. He pulled himself out, breathing hard. "You'll have to take over for a while," he said quietly, looking directly at me. I scrambled under, grabbed the crosscut, and began the push-pull action that bit into the trunk. Harder than I expected, I understood how he could be so breathless, but I was more surprised at my own ignorance. All the years we had come to these hills, it had been his pride to bring down the tree. I wondered what small aberration of the heart had made him stop, and what it had cost him to ask me, after thirty years of prideful watching, to finish the cut.

When the tree plumed over onto the hillside, we grabbed the trunk branches and lugged it down the slope. Together we lifted the heavy trunk into the pickup. Then we stood in the truck bed, up to our hips in evergreen. He grinned but said nothing, and looked over the white dreamlike acres that seemed to go on forever. But now I knew what he had known when he asked for help—they had a limit. There was a boundary to this long field, this farm that had always seemed endless, and a limit to strength, a limit to the dream of the day.

"Thanks for letting me do that," I said, trying to smooth any rough edges on this new territory between us. He looked at me and nodded. Back in the warm cab, scented with diesel and pine, we held hands all the way back to the river. It was snowing harder as the wind kicked up its ancient warning. He drove more slowly down the old roads.

Sauna

In every northland county, a few Nordic families (and some distinctly un-Nordic) still carry out the old tradition of sauna. For David and me, the winter has been blessed with visits to our friends' Sunday night community sauna in a shed-roofed, lantern-lit, hand built sweatbox of an edifice, a dark annex to the original homestead. Norm and Mimi's sauna is homey worship, a church of sorts, the liturgy of sweating through frayed towels. The small, bench-lined room is lit by a single lantern from a high window and the sauna stove's flickering glow. A wood-burning stove Norm bought from an old stove maker in the Upper Peninsula graces the corner. The rocks were hand-picked from our chilly Lake Michigan beach, and in the gray tray of the stove, those granite rounds rest like ancient eggs in a metal basket, incubating in a liturgy of heat. The cedar boards are smooth and dark with heat, recycled from some salvage job in Leland. The benches are stained from years of sweat and the light oils some people use like an anointing. This sauna's small anteroom shelves shoes and boots and opens onto a stone patio where people rest and cool between bouts with the heat.

Since adopting Leelanau County as homeland, we have learned to take sauna year-round, but sauna, I believe, never feels as good as in the dead of winter. Or, as Norm claims, in the *life of winter*. After a cold snap is best. After new snow is better. After a serious blizzard is sublime. And nothing so fulfills sauna's promise as that courageous roll in new snow after the intense heat of the inner sanctum. We have also come to believe it is why we have fewer colds and more resilience to these gray months.

On sauna nights, we crowd into the small room and sweat, sometimes talking, sometimes not. We catch up on news of the week or rest quietly, feeling the warmth take hold in this coldest of seasons. Through tired pores, perspiration squeezes out every toxin—from bad bourbon to our boss's petty remarks. Our small lives loosen, pour down our jaws and arms, slide in streams down our backs and torsos until, wrapped in soaked towels, we sit in puddles of forgotten hardships. Once, our friend Richard brought his Didgeridoo into the sauna and played through the steaming heat, the low drone a perfect accompaniment for the inner cleansing required for people to live well through Michigan winter. We were tied to Earth in that moment, to the oldest of the old, the Australian indigenous people's drone connecting us with dream song and desert soil. That deep and centered sound inside the sauna entered our ears, made a spirit pact with heat, breathing for the whole body. We felt the turning of the seasons in more ways than one.

Once, during a particularly hot sauna, when things in that room felt uptight from too much bad luck in our lives, we didn't realize how hot it had gotten, and we weren't paying attention to the temperature. We stayed and stayed until it opened everything, right down to our middle-aged hearts. On that winter night we talked the small and large hurts, through the green angers, *I never forgave her for lying*; curdled dreams, *I thought I could be a singer*; lost dog, *he was hit when I left the gate open*; death in the family, *she wouldn't tell us what she wanted*; a last good-bye, *I didn't know she would be deported*; an unpaid, unjust bill, *she made me pay to repair her wedding dress*; the dark side to an old love story, *the letters were burned before I could read them.* We sat there, confessing and confiding, culling our own darkness, flirting with how long we could take the hard-core heat of these truths that can be said no other way.

This is what rock heat does, this ritual that realigns us with the ancient volcanoes and ice spirits who made this baptism that lets human beings survive winter. In those hours, we replicate an ancient practice of survival. We let go of the coldness of our own experiences, the ones we cannot fully resolve, and we take on inner heat that holds for days, that allows us to see into the dark of our existence. It is the transition of heat from skin to the inner muscle that opens and reveals the truths we could not see in the light. It makes us so vulnerable, we cannot look each other in the eye, but watch the flagstones on the floor, the flicker of flames against the window, the steam that rises from the hot rocks. Not everyone feels this, but those who practice sauna deeply, we do.

Who knows how epiphany arrives?

When our faces have sweat so hard (or perhaps we have cried ourselves out), Mimi pours eucalyptus oil generously into a cup of ice water, and dumps it full force and without ceremony on the stones. The steam rockets off the stones. Ray screams, Jenny howls. We all find new voices as the heated menthol scorches away our various sins. This is a song we did not know before that moment. In each sauna, what we learn is that we will never sing it again, not with that same heat or heart. Each one is a different ritual, united by fire. We will return and hear it differently.

When we are at last quiet, someone in the room has sense enough to realize we have stopped sweating and that we could die of this. All seven of us rush into air so chill it freezes our lashes on the spot, turns our hair to ice strands. We never feel the cold. We flap our arms, watching as steaming, full-grown wings rise from our bodies, clean at last of the thick and ordinary evils of that spirit winter. We are light and transformed, ready at last for flight.

Kuieren

Through the fall and winter, calls had gone back and forth, checking up, checking in, one time hopeful, the next softly despairing. *She's down again. Hasn't been up for ten days. Labored breathing. Too thin to sustain life.* Finally, the call came on a Tuesday evening in February. My beloved aunt was gone, the services Saturday. I agreed to drive my parents to the funeral and graveside.

I didn't expect sunshine that morning in early February. Clouds had laden the skies on the Leelanau Peninsula for weeks, and I had dreaded another gray day, but that night had cleared, leaving hoarfrost and the rare champagne sun of mid-winter. We drove US-31's sun and shadow moments, looking out at the lace of pines lining the highway. I asked my dad, who had been inordinately quiet, to tell me more about my grandparents on his side, the people who had birthed him and my Aunt Minnie. When he couldn't, I realized the question was too imprecise. Instead, I asked him what sounds he most fondly remembered. His surprising answer—that they sang together, that Minnie had a good voice, and that grandpa would follow, and they would sing the old Dutch and Belgian ballads, and then as one memory leads on, he told me, "My dad would come home from church and change to work clothes, but it was Sunday, so he couldn't work. Instead, he would go on kuieren."

"What's that?" I asked. It's Dutch or Flemish, I know, just because it sounds like a swallowed growl. Dutch was spoken in my father's childhood home, among all of that generation. Both my grandparents spoke English with thick accents, and reverted to the old country's language whenever they could. Even though Dad was bilingual, he never pushed the language on us kids, wanting us fully assimilated. I wished then, and often now, that we had retained more of our origin language.

He had to think a minute. He had to translate in his head first. Finally, "It means something like wandering. Your grandpa would go outside and walk the fields, one after another, until he had covered all of his land." Both explanation and action rang true for our family. Like a genetic predisposition, we were all such walkers. We walked fields and roads, we were nightwalkers and early morning walkers. Garden walkers. Field walkers. It was in our blood, to wander over land, to take a look at the earth.

At the church, I thought about my father, my Uncle Joe, my Aunt Catherine and my Aunt Mary, the four remaining siblings of that generation, all sitting in a pew together, leaning close to each other. I saw the wide faces: Aunt Catherine's still-dark brows, my father's and uncle's sharp, hooked noses—all peasant stock. Sturdy and resourceful, aging as old apples. I looked around at some fifty cousins and second cousins, kneeling, murmuring the soft prayers. I watched old friends of the family bent in their winter coats with their bright scarves tucked under their collars, their eyes full of the patience farming can create in people open to it. I saw the younger ones turning in their seats, catching each other's eyes. Later. Later. For them always a later. They were still immortal.

I saw the blood lines carried out, the high and wide fore-head, the thick bridge between the brows, wide cheek bones and full mouths. I saw the protruding ears sprinkled through the descendants, the gray eyes and extraordinarily large hands coming to surface in every family. And always the big feet. Everywhere big feet. Something necessary to the migrating they had done, wandering back and forth over the lands and fields, even the ocean. Kuieren.

The procession to the cemetery led through more fields. This month, no snow, not even hard earth-frost, and the sun blazed that pale yellow light of winter onto the dark soil that had been plowed in the fall. The cars pulled off a blue highway into a two-track cemetery road and onto three level acres boundaried by a line of trees. There were no buildings to break the view, not a church, not a vault, not even storage for tools, just wide fields. My cousins and brothers climbed out of their cars, raised their faces and sniffed the air like animals, like wolves or wild dogs, scenting. People spoke out, commanding each other, "Smell the dirt, smell that soil. Maybe an early spring, ya think?" The winter sun came straight down on us as we stood in the cold and prayed for the dead, one of our own, but we kept looking out over the fields, looking at the dirt, the loam, all of us wishing we could walk it just to ease our grief, for the comfort of the wander.

And then the prayers were finished, the coffin was low-ered, and we drifted back to the cars where we stood for long minutes, crushing broken fern and frozen geranium. We all avoided each other's eyes, looked out toward the empty fields, corn or straw stubble. And then it happened. As I watched, my sister stepped out toward the edge of the cemetery and began the short walk into the field where she lifted her head to the wind. Then my brothers and father also stepped away,

away from the plots that held the ancestors, the neighbors, the warriors lost in the wars, the plots that held my aunt's remains. They left the plotted spaces and walked onto the one thing they knew for certain in life, those beloved and long fields.

The Meal

I had driven too many miles, had been too long on the road as a Poet-in-Residence for a series of spring visits to school systems throughout Great Lakes states. I was a practicing poet, and an experienced teacher, but the best of lesson plans had been shattered by unruly classes and ill-timed lunch breaks. Fire and tornado drills—really, two in the same day? Sometimes teachers didn't prepare students. Or themselves, *who are you again*? Sometimes they abandoned the classrooms entirely, leaving me with students as sullen as parking lot puddles. Sometimes I simply failed to bring the right poems, poems that were real enough, poems that mattered. When their interest flagged, mine did also. I was tired, I was losing my touch, my patience, and felt off kilter. When I finally finished the last school visit late one afternoon, I didn't have time to drive all the way back to Leelanau, but I dreaded yet another nondescript mid-state hotel without David.

There was one place. My sister Marijo's Michigan home was halfway up Michigan's west coast and halfway home. We hadn't seen each other for weeks.

One of many "homes" of this adult life is my sister's country farmhouse, surrounded by barns and gardens, filled with dogs, cats, three exuberant kids, and her delightful husband. I don't see her as much as I'd like because I'm on the road so much, but when I do, I am delighted with them and their culture, country work mixed with hunting, fishing, and playing in the wild. A quick call and I'm on US-31, driving into north country, past Muskegon, past Montague, driving to the town I left decades ago, to Hart, where my sister stayed and raised her family. As I hit the exit ramp, the sky suddenly expands, the air clears and my shoulders drop like bricks.

My sister's home is a place in the sun, one full of the vocabulary of soil and harvests, all laced with the rich teasing of family I had almost forgotten. I wheel in at six, a couple of hours ahead of sunset, to be greeted by their cat and beagle, and my six-foot sister, Marijo, running toward the car with mesh bags popping out of her Carhartt pockets. Those open weave bags are used for only one harvest.

"You're kidding; it's too early." I tell her.

"We'll find some." She exudes excitement.

"It's too cold." Isn't it?

"But it's been rainy and humid, and today the sun—" She hugs me, smelling of open air, soil, and garlic. "Come quick."

And before I can change shoes, I'm being tugged by her boys into the woodlot.

Much has been written about morel hunting, but for those who haven't hunted these oddly shaped, roughly textured, and rustically flavored mushrooms, the thrill of the first spring hunt is matched by few quests in existence. My week's work with unwilling writers who knew more than I did about everything in the world begins to slink into scrub thickets beside these woodsy paths.

Here is a poem of discovery, of sly jokes, the humor of mushrooms. Hide-and-Go-Seek. Peak-a-Boo. I bend over the damp leaf mulch under old pines and oaks on the hillsides. Hard at first, hunting is a sixth sense (like riding a bike) that comes back after you've foraged for a while. I'm not good at it, but Marijo is. She puts in the time, learning to see them. Like other hidden moments, these "shrooms" sneak up, and just as you are about to give up, their slim caps rise from the scuffed dirt at your feet. *Here we are, now we're not.* Within moments the kids are finding these small nuggets of unassuming fungus, a gourmet's gold. We hunt until the sack is full. With enough for a meal, we head home, chattering and rough-housing in the paths, laughing and competing to tell the best stories about how the world is full of bright strangeness and the hunting is fine.

Back at the house, John, Marijo's lanky husband is cracking a dark home brew beer.

Marijo asks, "Did you get some?"

"I did indeed," John replies with mock reverence and nods toward a small crate on the worn counter. He lifts the towel ceremoniously and I gasp.

"The first picks of the year. I walked over ten acres to find this much." He chooses a few green stalks and we sniff the rich green of fresh Michigan asparagus, one of the best kept secrets in the culinary world.

Overshadowed by high production agribusinesses of California and Mexico, Michigan's asparagus was once only sold fresh in Great Lakes area grocery chains and then only by those few merchants who want to share a vegetable treasure overlooked by those who don't know any better. Now it's different; it's coveted as soon as the season comes one. Michigan asparagus stock grows heavier, more robust stalks, with richer flavor than the thin "pansy" asparagus shipped from western states and supposedly prized—for what, stringiness? And these, the first pickings of the year are the tenderest, sweetest of the season. Here is a poem rising from childhood flavors, from good work in a spring field.

Over the raucous talk, the next phase of the meal unfolds. The boys bundle into heavy jackets, pulling on layers. Marijo hunts for flashlight batteries, and John calls friends. Trout and walleye season are only a few days old, and their "fish fever" has not cooled. I wonder at their confidence, their certainty of the catch, but though I am already hungry, I am more than willing to wait for this rare mesh of flavors.

A short drive down Bridge Road, a hike through trees, and we are shuffling through the sand to the south pier of the Pentwater harbor. As dark moves in, the wind picks up and blows a few clouds east. The last dregs of sun sliver over Lake Michigan, the lake where I am always a child. Once on the pier, we discover clusters of fisher folk forming another small culture—not writers, not teachers, not recalcitrant learners—but lovers of the lake and night air, these night fishers. The evening air fills with calls back and forth over the water, bits of news, a shout for nets. Chilly gusts puff against us; the deep waters chatter against the boulders of the breakwater. Here, the smelt dippers, salmon and trout fishers gather to cast in the legal harbor territory. Here, we greet long-lost friends, older fisher folk, wild-eyed kids. When the dark comes full on and the cold bites, Marijo slyly pulls a bottle of Hot Damn, cheap cinnamon schnapps, from her pocket and passes it. People gasp and snort at the taste, then warm up, as much from her generosity as from the liquor.

John pulls in two big walleye, and his oldest, Zack, lands a small trout. "Plenty," Marijo announces and we abandon the rugged shoreline just as the stars begin to show for real. This is a poem of fins and raw flesh, of the silver coined scales flashing on the knife, the poem of plenty.

At ten that night, a meal is served in my sister's crowded kitchen, a poem that can happen only in the living of it, and only with the convergent luck of certain harvests. Onto chipped stoneware, John slips fresh walleye fillets, pan-fried in herbed breading. Jo sluices on fresh morels sautéed in garlic and beer. We heap the steamed asparagus with real butter. There is warm wheat bread if we need it, cheap Rose if we want it. The meal consists of what this good land and new season have given us: mushrooms from the woods, asparagus from the fields, walleye from the lake. I have travelled far from the noon of writerly frustration to this evening verse, stanzas of renewal with my sister and her family. Here, a poem to make me whole again.

A Simple Practice

March still feels like the dead of winter, cold and dark with a day or two of deception laced in. Despite the fact that we are nearly past the equinox, dawn is still late, and here I am wrapped in layers, opening the front door with a cup of hot tea, headed nowhere. This is an essay, I warn you, about nothing.

I settle on the stoop, the step freshly swept by my more conscientious husband. I sit and stare at the winter garden, it's only points of interest some dry hydrangea, the scrap of rhododendron shrub, the dark stems of the trumpet vine twisting over the crust of hard snow. I watch the dark trunks of a hundred trees sway in the mixed-mood wind, a creak here and there, punctuating the shift of air. I sit and sip, and feel the warmth of the tea all the way down, and I watch my breath drift over the hot rim and disappear. The neighbor's dog lopes down the driveway as she always does on our day off, comes scruffing up to nose my fuzzy slippers, then with a look of puzzlement as if she wondered if there would be purpose, meaning, a ball to chase (there is not), she burrows under the porch.

I have come out into the cold with a hot drink. For the cold. For the feel of heat in my hands, against my face. For what it does to me in this busy life I lead. It changes nothing, this ritual; there is no momentum. It would be boring—it is boring except...

The first time, I was twelve. On a bitter winter day, without permission, I took a tiny thermos of hot chocolate to the beach and sat on a drift log. I was alone and just old enough to want time on my own, just old enough to sense that reverie, when one could get it, was important. My mind at that time was trying to keep up with the whirlwind of my newly grown body and its commitment to changing. The heated drink leaning its taste against the cold calmed me—though I could not have said that then. What was I doing? Nothing. But then, those thoughts drifted away and I was left staring at the clipped, sharp-edged waves, aware of the sound of the rough ice spinning against itself, the wind close and unruly, and then the warm contrasting liquid slipping down, the warmth on my fingers, the heat rising close to the skin on my face. The cold wind.

Another time, I escaped to the woods, sat on deadfall, let the cold swirl around me, let the creamy drink warm me. I thought about the boy I had a crush on, the way my mother didn't want me to dress, how I hated these new breasts I had been given during the summer's growth spurt. If I held the cup just so it pressed into that space just below my clavicle, warmth spread through my body. The real though unimportant worries of a young girl slipped into the moss at my feet. I was present. To what? Nothing. Or to the whole world in which I lived, its contrasts, its harshness against these gentile flavors of comfort. Storm and warm. Wind and tea.

Even then, I knew this was a landscape of small contrasts, a cusp I could balance inside of, a place where nothing happened.

Later, the practice took the form of running away. On that noisy, communal farm where I grew up, I could pour an insulated cup of something hot and steal behind the house to stare over the frost-edged orchard. I could sneak into the chilled and still barn lofts where, if I stayed unobtrusive, I wouldn't be put to work but could listen to the distant voices of my brothers and fathers and other men as they worked with animals or machines. Once I climbed a high hunter's blind in winter, balancing my first cup that had an anti-spill lid, and watched wild dogs run a deer over far hills. I did not see the end. As far as I know, nothing happened.

I still carry dark-roast coffee, herbal fusions, toddies or tea and go out into the cold. I set some warm interior, some heated liquid against some cold exterior stiffness: the beach in snow, a windy pier in November, a bench in a quiet park after the first hard frost. It must be cold. There must be a cup of hot cider, a pint of tea with a touch of brandy, or steaming coffee. Warm thought against cold beauty. Nothing happens. Lately, on our trips further up north to our rustic Canadian cabin, on those cold mornings when my husband valiantly stirs coals and nurses a fire into being, I wrap myself in blankets and carry the dark coffee out onto the frozen lake, walking on stilled water with the heat of a hot drink melting my mind, steam rising before me like a spirit. I stand there, holding the cup, and I know that nothing happens, nothing at all that you or I can see. In this small insignificant holding, everything is contained. Everything happens.

Dunes: Three Tales

Over time, I have fallen in love with dunes, specifically the Sleeping Bear Dunes National Lakeshore on the west coast of Leelanau County in Northwest Lower Michigan. There are times when I must "go to the dunes" or perhaps more to the point, I must *Be There*. At first, it stemmed from my fascination with geography. The dunes, a malleable desert, shift empty sand into living shapes, contours of moving particles—these drifts are never the same one season to another. The arid ecosystem is a landscape both simple and complex, functional but poetic—the way a dune can look no other way than what it does and yet it calls out for comparisons—flank of a golden lion, resting brown bear, ghost of sand. There is always something muscular, ancient, and utterly malleable about the dunes. It will not look the same tomorrow. I feel like myself there.

Another reason is story. Or rather, stories. Even before I lived here, I had heard the creation tale of the dunes, the Ojibway Sleeping Bear myth. It touched me so deeply that I learned it and retell it by heart at every bonfire. It is a simple story, but holds subtle and powerful complications. Forced by famine and fire, a great she-bear (apparently living in Wisconsin) leads her cubs to the shore of Lake Michigan and attempts to cross the lake to the shoreline of Michigan. Though she helps the cubs, they are weakened by the long

178

journey. After many days, she pulls herself onto the bluffs and calls to the cubs still in the waters, but they are too tired, and they sink under the waves. The She-bear stays on the shore forever, watching and waiting until she falls asleep under the golden sand. Finally the great spirit transforms the cubs into two magnificent islands, and names them after himself, North Manitou and South Manitou. When I think into the She-Bear narrative, I feel the contradictions—that she sleeps in peace but also watches eternally. A paradox. When I imagine how her cubs have become islands, I think of shape-shifting, its beauty and mystery. To be two things at once, to be and not to be. I touch the nature of longing. Her cubs-turned-island are visible, earth-now, but untouchable.

Then there's a practical side to the story. I had always assumed that the Sleeping Bear was the entire open dune-land of the National Lakeshore; that since the tale was a mythical narrative, it was also mythical in its size and that the whole, huge expanse of shifting sands, some seventy thousand acres, was the Sleeping Bear, Mishe Mokwa. All that open sand must be the golden blanket that covered her, majestic as the range itself, as she waited for her cubs.

The actual logistics surprised me. The Sleeping Bear was a specific dune, a hilltop high point covered with dark foliage that dropped down the high west face of the dune like the head and arms of a great bear, nose in the middle. It was a particularly important landmark to sailors in the early part of the last century, its visibility a point of location in the treacherous Manitou Channel. When I realized that there was a time that the dark foliage could be pointed to and named as a point of reference, the story took on an even more eerie reality. There had once been forest, a specific place, that looked like an enormous sleeping bear, high on the bluffs. Where was it now?

It took me years to understand and to find the place. That one-and-only dune had become a blow-out, a place the wind had worked into until the center was hollow, and the soil no longer anchored more than the simplest grasses. Instead, the blow-out revealed a system of once buried ghost trees that stand like the bones of the majestic creature it was said to house. The single dune that represented her had disappeared in the wind. Though I am not a superstitious person, I had to ask: was the destruction of the dune symbolic of her leaving us? When I expressed this fear to a grizzled artist friend whose family had lived in this area since the settlement era, he told me not to worry, that in fact the dunes were one of the few places where the old ones still live.

"The old ones?" I watched him make a pattern of stones and driftwood on the beach.

"The old ones, spirits mostly. You know, spirits of trees and rivers that no longer exist, and great animals, and people who were born and died here, and others we don't even know, even more ancient."

"They live in the dunes?"

"They lived all over Leelanau. This was a place that never had a lot of industry, you know? Just small farms. The old ones felt comfortable staying. They could live with a tractor plowing down grass a couple times a year, or even the orchard work; there were woods to go into. They were okay if there wasn't some engine running twenty-four-seven."

"But now?" I didn't voice my skepticism.

"Most of them have left, you know, because it's too developed, and nobody is sensitive to them. But if you walk quietly in the wood lots, you'll still feel a few."

My friend is maybe a little crazy. After all, he saves old bones and spends hours collecting driftwood and stones which he sets together on the beaches as art installations.

He grins roguishly, reading my doubt.

"So, where'd the old ones go?" I ask.

"Most just leave. But some can't yet, they still have business here. So they move to the dunes. It's pretty crowded in there now. That's why no one can live there. That's why the sand moves. That's why the sand slides, now and then the bluff just lets go. All those spirits."

I'm chuckling, "And I thought it was just the She-Bear up there."

"She's there. Others too."

"How do you know all this?" I ask.

"Oh, don't believe everything you hear." He laughs, but looks straight at me before he goes back to his work, placing a stone shaped like a broken moon into the curved arm of a driftwood branch.

* * *

His story of the Old Ones intrigues me as much as the story of the She-Bear. I have a lawless imagination, and it is sensitive to place. Entering the dunes, following the nearly invisible dune buggy trail to the ghost forest, using other paths to the shoreline, I wander too. Here, in this low draw where two dunes come together, is this the ghost of an ancient river, its currents still visible in the sand ripples? Or here, where the warm air rises in a sweet-scented updraft, the spirit of some healing plant; or here, the calculating scream of the red-tail hawk on the hunt.

I go to the dunes, enter the place where there are only wind-words, where skin becomes more sensitive to sun, temperature, moisture and, reading these forces as best I can, I walk for hours on and beneath the bluffs, listening to the blue muffle of water on rounded rocks. Am I walking the skin and bones of something stilled but alive? In the end, it is hard to say what I feel because it is so big, so unlanded in a way that still connects me deeply with Place.

Perhaps it is that feeling of mystery that leads me to ask, very tentatively, an indigenous storyteller if she can tell me more about the dunes. Of course, she wants to know why I want to know and why I'm asking her. I tell her: I am trying to find my way deeper into place-love. I am spending a lot of time on the dunes. I've learned some of both the geographical and recent cultural histories, but I would be grateful for stories from *before* settlement history. I am trying to be respectful, yet my question is contradictory—I am also asking what is happening there now, something that I feel and cannot name. I don't want to invade her sacred stories, but if I am to help care for a place, even in a small way, could I be told something more of how it has come to be. She is as cautious answering as I am in my question. "Yes," she admits. "There is another story of the dunes. It is told in a great four-day ceremony."

I am afraid to ask, but she knows how to say it. "I can tell you a little, the part you could find in books if you look hard enough. That's no secret, though the ceremony is."

And so she tells me what she can. The gist is that the dunes were the site of a great battle between the Blue Thunderbird and the Red Underwater Serpent, two equal forces, one committed to air and light, one to the underworld of deep water. Their battle raged a long time, may not yet be resolved, and may continue until the two creatures are transformed into one. A feathered serpent who both flies and swims. There is more to this, but my friend draws her boundary there, and I understand by what is unsaid as much as by what is said. I must be careful and respectful, but I think I can draw a tentative personal inference from her telling, though it will not necessarily be her truth: the dunes are the grounds (both spiritual and ecological) on which the battles happened and continue to happen. The forces are contiguous with our time; the dunes are not empty. These battles may not be dualistic, not a win or lose, not even a combat in the sense we use that word, but may instead be a mutually essential struggle; a complex and existential means for transformation.

As I walk down the high dune to the point south of Glen Haven, I imagine them rising, creating the red-threaded sunset, the pearly smoke of a lake surface. From my own place in my culture, I think about what she has given, this story gift that is more than story, that is also a way into place-being. Often, I have brought my internal battles here, to sort out their various sides, to site the best way from many ways, to transform a problem into something more under-standable, to let an interior conflict work its way through me as I walk. And finally, though there has been no conscious resolution, I feel the troubles of my self-centered universe become transformed, something that is, if the metaphor can be extended, both scaled and feathered, both of air and water, pluming like rain feathers in wind.

At the same time, I can hear my friend laughing. "You people," my friend would say. "Can't you ever see that all this two-bit psychology is all about you?" And I would smile, knowing she's right. But even as she is chastising me, I know she feels reverence for the dunes. Lots of us do, no matter from what culture we hail. Simply put, the dunes create spirituality of place, different from conventional religion or Western tradition, and different still from the pastiche of thought that permeates and passes for spirituality in much of new age culture. That said, perhaps the dunes bring us closest to the landscape and practice of the desert monks, the hermits who walked away from their villages to live in the emptiness (the desert!) because it brought them closer to God and ironically, the natural world—and thus taught them lessons: their limitations, boundaries, vulnerabilities. Though our history reveres these eccentrics as informal saints, they were people struggling with transformation. Perhaps the desert brought them closer to their own humanity, their commitment held in the tensions created by scriptural metaphor and survival. Does something like that happen when we walk the dunes?

Perhaps, when we listen respectfully to stories we are generously offered by elders and by the Anishinaabe, we touch the body of a great She-Bear, are brushed by wings mad with thunder, grazed by a serpent made of water, and looped into the dreams of the old ones. Perhaps, if we stilled our raucous minds, we could feel the complexity of the stories, the nature of story itself surging under the lines of sand drift, stirring the imagination in a way that is necessary for change, for transformation.

Beach Glass

My dear friend, Bronwyn, first taught me about beach glass. Her family has, for generations, owned the white lattice-windowed cottage set in a locust grove north of Empire. I go there often to be with her good company. We are sitting on the sand at what I fondly call Bronwyn's Beach—an isolated stretch of the Sleeping Bear Dunes National Lakeshore between Empire and North Bar Lake—when she picked up what I assumed was a tiny stone. This blue-tinted bit of translucence rolled in her hand like a small clearing on a hazy day, rounded and smooth as any beach stone, but the color was brighter blue, and the weight lighter than any beach stone I had ever seen. "Look," she said. "It's become beautiful." And then she told me how in her family, collecting beach glass was an old tradition, how they prized beach glass above other beach treasures. And I remembered how on the sills of her cottage, these tiny findings were tucked among the fine ceramics and books. Beach glass. She told me finding a piece brings good luck, "Because it's been changed from trash into a lovely thing."

Since that day many years ago, I too search for beach glass. There is something astonishingly hopeful about discovering these gemlike chips among the gray and blue granite pebbles that cover our beaches. The glass is harder to find now, rarer because more people have discovered it, and also because we're thankfully moving away from the days when the lake was a trash barrel for glass. Now it is the search that matters. A search for old beach glass makes me walk more slowly, bending, scanning the swash for these delicate capsules of translucent light among the dark gloss and drama of the beach stones. These pieces are usually softer looking, paler, sometimes pastel as early dawn. When I find a worn shard tossed among the Petoskeys and quartz, and I see the sun play on the green or blue or clear matte finish, I remember Bronwyn's words.

This is a remnant of something once functional, then broken, then sharply dangerous, the carapace of some human made shard which could sting or bite. I remember what this beach glass might have been—a shattered Gallo or Mogen David bottle, a clear pickle jar, maybe the broken neck of Milk of Magnesia, the amber of Mrs. Butterworth or now forgotten beers. Sometimes I find colors about which I can't guess. What was the lovely amethyst, the almost peach? Something older? A vase? A rare stained-glass window lost from the captain's cabin of a tall ship? Now, they are tiny artifacts of what they once were. The beach glass hints at tales I'll never know but I can dream, imagining their stories in my head. Finding a piece gentles the buzzing, the frantic business of living.

When I need to quiet my restless brain, I go back to those beaches and look for glass. It is not easy to make time, what with work and family, but it is necessary. As I walk, I remember. The glass comes from sand, was made into something useful—a container, a window, and then it was destroyed or discarded into the waves of Lake Michigan. Now the lake has done its smooth work. The currents have tossed them; they have lost sharp edges, are remade into a rounded-off glimmer, lovely and simple, not dangerous. The shards are on their way to becoming merely particles, and for a little while we watch the good work of the waves, catch their muted light, hold a lake's artwork in our palms, drop their misty colors into our pockets, remembering perhaps how permanent they once seemed, how transient they are; we are.

Stone Courtesy

For a long time that summer, the site remained intact.

If you were beach walking, the formations rose suddenly from the edge of rough shoreline half way between Empire Beach to Otter Creek Beach. I'd been picking my way through a particularly stony section of shore when I looked up to discover four stones cairns, each about three feet high, set in a row parallel to the beach, and surrounded by a circle of gray and darker granite stone. The cairns, built of piled flat stones common to this whole area, were set without mortar and were capped by large pink stones so perfectly balanced I thought each must have been pinned or glued, but when I looked closely I realized—this was art and equilibrium.

The four formed a gateway to a stone pyramid, set further up the beach, about four feet tall and four feet square, facing west, and again built of the flat stones balanced on each other and set without mortar. In the center of these two formations a wooden stump, set in front of the pyramid, invited the visitor to sit and watch. I did, feeling a sliver of adventure and wonder. It must have taken weeks to stack these, one by one. What was the story? Who built it and why?

Through late summer and early fall I visited the cairns. I also met dozens of people going to and coming from the stones. I asked many but no one knew for sure. I heard that the builder was from Wisconsin, not Michigan. Another person said a family with children helped him. According to another, the man had begun the project in early summer, had worked several days a week, gathering the flat stones, assembling and stacking the stones as tribute for a woman who was battling breast cancer, creating a healing site. Each time I stumbled onto someone who could tell me something, they spoke in the general terms that we use when we may not know all the facts, but we are responding to an idea we want to believe in. People recognized that impressive act of discipline, a personal commitment to walk that mile each day to spend hours moving stones. It had to be an effort of will to carry and place and balance the stones. It would have to be motivated by something beyond artistic drive or whimsy, by something like friendship and perhaps, even love.

And nobody ever hurt the pyramid or the cairns. Hundreds of people like myself made that pilgrimage on their days off, matching my common reverence. All through the remarkable days of a tourist rush, no one had broken or marred or interfered with the development of the towers or pyramid. Instead they had developed an ordinary and kind story about the place and the maker, as though they needed to honor the builder as much as the building. Sometimes I would find people there meditating, sometimes sitting on the stump or the sand or even behind the pyramid, lining up the sunset with the tip of it.

I think the site appealed to the people who walked our beaches because the cairns evoked a balance, a gentility from the silence of rocks. We were better because of the stones. Our imaginations took us to a place beyond whimsey, to some source of the sacred. We recalled Stonehenge, Newgrange, the pueblos of the West. Our own invented tales. For months, nothing happened there, people respected the endeavor and the beauty that was the result. That reverence for place, for the beauty of balance, a soft awe protected the site. No one did anything but add the occasional stone.

I never heard exactly why the site was created, if it was true about the family or the woman with breast cancer, or a love tribute. In the end, it didn't matter. We all brought our own stories to the place.

Late in fall, a hard westerly storm tore through the region and all but one of the cairns collapsed in the onslaught of eight-foot waves. But the pyramid stood, its western side facing the lake, the setting sun, its implacable flat stones linked in a balancing act between natural forces and the lovely courtesy of people who, for a short time, found a site that inspired wonder and not destruction.

Then, after the tourists abandoned the park, the rangers dismantled the pyramid, saying there was a law that no one could build a permanent structure within the parameters of the park. Permanent? Really? Now, when I walk, I come to the one place where in the sand, the layers of flat stones are scattered more densely than in other parts of the beach. If you stop there, a sadness will rise.

Fallings

Three off-season thunderstorms in three days and after each, the *fallings*. As if the weight of rain, of downpour itself finally throws off the delicate balance of the standing dead, their dried-up roots grasping freeze-dried soil, and whatever was that poise that kept them upright for so long abandons them. In that cold silence after storm, in their slow tree time, they let go. In contrast to the time they stood, the time it took to die, they fall fast, crashing and popping through still living trees, a crackling that calls me out of doors, searching: which one, which one this time? Trees fall, yes, but so often now that I've begun to call them *fallings*. A dramatic verb turn-coating to a noun. The tree is not falling, instead it's *a falling*. An act unto itself. I go in search of the one who fell.

Usually, the *falling* is an ash, now almost gone due to the Emerald Ash Borer. Our ten-acre wood lot once held twenty-percent ash trees, now all are standing dead due to the infestation. Those words too touch me: *standing dead.* And provide paradox—for even though the ash are standing dead, they offer a boon to our woodpecker population, especially that bossy pileated who delves into the bark like a machine, despite that the bird looks like some pre-historic dinosaur dressed for the theater.

But after these storms, the remaining *standing dead* become *fallings*.

191

With the help of a tree service, each year we've removed as many standing dead as we can afford, launching with a circle nearest our house which happens to perch in the middle of these ten woodlot acres. From protecting the structure, we've slowly worked outward, trying to prevent fallings doing damage to the living maples. We never thought, when we built decades ago, that we'd have to think of the fallings. At that time, the woodlot seemed healthy. But with each year, afflictions increased: white birch left us first, then the ash, now the beech. I've learned to listen for that sudden crack echoing over our ravine, the plunging rip through still living branches. It hurts. Only the maples seem to be holding their own. For now.

This time, an impressive elder beech, an elegant tree, sprawling over the road. News spreads fast as neighbors try to leave for jobs via the road. Already, the chainsaws are launching their bite. I walk out to see branches flailing to the side, to catch the waft of sawdust as men work their trucks and chains. They clear quickly and efficiently, but decide to call a tree service for the big stuff. I look at the winterish sky, feel the absence of the great creature. Still.

"It's beech," I whisper to David.

Then my beloved David, as if reading my mind, asks if we can take side logs for fire wood before the service comes. We may. It is some comfort. Beech are shorter lived than maples; they often grow up hollow, and some people call them junk trees. But I love their creamy gray bark, their peculiar rustle, the way those hollows offer housing for other creatures, and most of all, that after falling, dried beech is priceless heat in the wood stove.

Which is how, on a chill-puckered day, I come to be bucking up that tree with my husband. Though I regularly help David split wood, I haven't done that lift and haul, tote and toss of wet logs in a sloppy ditch for a long time. In minutes we are both soaked, covered with tree debris and cold mud. Saw dust clings to my hair, and my glasses fog. When we stop to rest, I study the severely splintered trunk, too shattered to count rings, but on a side log, I count 100 rings before the center hollows. I'm sad to lose this elder, sad to see the new emptiness in our winter sky, gray where its canopy once latticed the clouds.

But right now, I am identifying with that bossy pileated woodpecker, finding sustenance in loss. Those logs will crackle—because nothing crackles in a woodstove quite like beech does, and no other log seems to throw the heat a beech log will. The terrible falling will be balanced with this small warmth, with the percussive sparking that backbeats winter wind on a frost-bitten night. I know the fallings will end, and in that silence, I am part of and witness to a terrible change. What becomes of us, when our trees stop filling the sky? Do we rise in heat? How do we transform? I think of beech in the woodstove, sparking a December night like stars in a box. I think of this as a cold sun breaks through, pressing into the open spaces with a sharp and stunning light.

October

Decades ago under a canopy of maples, the sky, strung with the half-turned leaves, threatened rain on a motley collection of old tables, bedstands with fancy but scratched headboards, leather trunks, and boxes of life's debris. A wide green lawn scraped with ruts: the workers had dragged the blocky furniture over the once tidy grass. I had stumbled on an auction sale out in Leelanau County. I was at that stage in life where I still needed some basic furniture, but I didn't have much money. The whole worn out look of the place promised good bargains, and I was desperate to take advantage.

Even in weather this muted, October is made of that rarified air you only get after first frost, but before the really hard ones close everything down, and you must stare November in the eye. Something in October is all denial. In October, everything that is green becomes touched with a verb all the trees are saying aloud. You can hear it in the way the wind wings through them, but you don't believe it, seduced by the color into forgetting the ends of things.

Young as I was, I didn't sense the truth. Or at least not all of it.

But a country auction, stacked and paraded on the lawn, is one of the truth tellers of time. Not many folks wandered among the goods, and most of those seemed interested in the farm equipment. I could tell the household items wouldn't bring much. And I could tell by the way items had been placed in boxes, so that one good thing hid among a lot of junky things, there wasn't much left of the place. But that one good thing, a good old thing, was glazed with wear that showed from long handling, from the very lines in your palms, the lines that mapped your life. I had to pull myself away from all that, to not be lured into buying that kind of item, even though when I lifted it, I could feel time thrumming through it. I had rooms to fill and a young life. I was not to be lured away from denial: life went on forever. I needed a cheap dresser.

There it was, next to the broken picket fence, a high boy, six drawers topped with cracked but filigreed mirror, glass beveled and just a little wavy, in that old dark check of the original finish that's been through everything a half dozen generations can throw at it. There, among four more modern dressers, two oak tables and one large old-fashioned ice box that the antique dealers would scarf up, my dresser, a good ole highboy. I couldn't let on because gosh, I only had three twenties in my purse and maybe no one would notice this old piece if I pretended not to, so I wandered, forced to stare into those boxes while I waited, back to truth and denial packed together.

Truth: That a pair of baby shoes set with a dozen flowered hankies, some that look hand embroidered, will never go to a good home and be worn again.

Denial: The sun will be this bright and mottled wonder forever, or at least every October.

Truth: That package of bean seeds, tucked into a cast iron fry pan, blackened and heavy, will never be viable.

Denial: The hot coffee I gratefully buy from the women at the folding tables where they tell me the name of the farm, will always be hot, will always taste this good against my cold mouth.

Truth: The farm is being sold for development.

Denial: That in the box with three cracked patent leather purses and three matching pair of high heel shoes, and one pair of saddle shoes, there will be one pair in my size. Still, I take note of the saddle shoes.

And then the auctioneer begins his song, his patter, his liturgy of money and loss.

Sold: the hankies, the fry pan, the high heels, the land.

I stand in the stunning light and don't let the truth in until after I have to raise my number to bid for the dresser. I bid higher than I should for the high boy that will stand in my own bedroom, filigree mirror distorting the future. By then I want a thing, an object by which to remember the contradictions of this day, its muted beauty falling among the lost things, the maple a blaze in my eyes as I struggle to drag the dark dresser back across the lawn and tie it into the trunk of my car with clothesline. After that, I walk back through the tattered remains of the day to hear the last of the man's song, and I discover that some buyer abandoned the saddle shoes on the trampled grass. I pick them up, study them, thinking just maybe they'll fit. A gray-haired lady with a hankie in her hands who has been sitting on the porch the whole time calls out, "Take them dear, put some more wear on them before they give out."

And in that moment, I see myself in her, and the maple wind rises and some of the big branches do like they do sometimes, they let go all at once, and I feel my face gone wet with October.

The Long Fields

Every time I go home to what is now Oomen Farms, a fully incorporated agribusiness now run by my brothers, my father, who still goes to work there every day, asks, "Do you want to take a crop tour?"

A crop tour is what it says, a tour of the crops, the fields. We don't walk anymore because the fields now are spread across the county, fields scattered among many townships. The acreage spreads wide, quilt blocks, patches apart. Crop tours are a way for farmers to check in with each field as if it were a living person.

I almost forgot the last time we did this.

* * *

We climb into the truck and my mother, who can no longer ride in the old trucks because of her bad back, hands us paper bags, and says, "While you're at it, bring me some green beans and fresh corn." The added purpose of every crop tour is to pick fresh vegetables for her, or for me, because god knows I cannot possibly have a decent fresh market where I insist on living. And even if I could get decent produce, it would not taste as good as the corn, tomatoes, zucchini, the very air from the farm. The latter part is true.

However, the real purpose of a crop tour is for my dad and me to simply be together. Sometimes we talk, but it's truncated.

Look at that field, good soil, that one.

Storm last week took out that old tree. In a year, good fire wood.

They put in a garden at church, ya know? Didn't have good dirt though.

Everything is *good*. Solidly. Not outstanding or excellent or terrible. Things are good or they are not. It's a stable mode of judgement. But a lot of what passes between us now is not talk, good or not, but rather the most companionable silence I know.

Even in the face of change, there's not much to say.

As we tool the big Chevy pickup onto the original 140 acres, it is not the same. The old barn is gone, replaced by the sprawling pole barns which house a million dollars' worth of equipment and again as much in seeds, herbicides, pesticides, and the equipment needed to fix equipment. The farmhouse is still there but it has new vinyl siding, that nondescript taupe color preferred now, and the wild spirea has been replaced by nursery shrubs. That said, the big silver maple stands, over a hundred and twenty years old now, and the wide sloping yard still runs to the gravel road, though the long grass-bound driveway has been fixed in chipped stone. It is a "good" working farm and the improvements prove that it is thriving. This is where I grew up, but I don't always recognize it.

My father is still invested, still goes to the "shop" every day, a crude office in the huge pole barn, where now he and my brothers gather with the crews, or the supervisors of the crews, and make the plans, and send the workers out to the fields and make it all happen in the green. I know this is a BIG thing my brothers are doing. There is no other word for it, this farming. It sprawls with immensity. My brothers, in this deeply flawed and demanding profession, feed people, or rather feed a market that feeds people. It is a strange system, practical and yet inefficient, developed in a complex interaction of government and bureaucracy and seed companies and processors and soil. So my father goes to the pole barn office daily; he worries about how much money his sons spend, how much equipment costs, how much fertilizers and pesticides and herbicides cost.

He doesn't have the energy for the hard labor or the calculations anymore, but what everyone knows—there are few in the county who can look at a field as he does, the long and short of it, especially the long of it. Because he knows that these fields, despite the compromises of contemporary farming, despite the application of chemistry and all kinds of science, are, in their unpredictability, more like old gods, gods spread wide with their own strange wisdom, part of a thing unto themselves, no matter what is being applied to them. And not until I enter the fields do I find my connection again, do I feel both his attention and my homing. The smell of green is the grace of my life, and weather, being "outside" in a field, smelling of growth and roots, is the true blood line.

He says, "Now, look at that." Look at that, which is what he does. He looks, studies, lets in the light. Studies again. He reads the land as I read a book.

The crop tour moves from one field to another, from hundred-plus acre plots to twenties. We drive under the arms of monster irrigation rigs, over acreage of pine plantations, into plots of smaller fields where experimental crops are being "winded" by helicopters. In every field we stop, we pick something green or yellow or orange. Depending on the season, my father points out this field of bright squash, brings an armload of carrots, tosses in some cabbage, broccoli, and even late fruit into the bags and boxes. I will carry these away to my kitchen. I will give to friends and make dinners for days with soft peaches, tiny zucchini, sweet corn, and lush tomatoes. There is a sense of luxury in all this food, more than I will ever need. It is the true good that I never felt as a child, this abundance. I thought it would always be there, that I could go back and touch it. Now, only on visits. Only on these crop tours, sometimes with a six pack.

* * *

The last crop tour we took together was in May, too early for anything but the asparagus harvest. It was a crop tour taken in the innocence that comes from not looking at numbers and the processes of time, looking only at the grace. The good. We picked the spears and then went looking for something else.

That day, Dad drove us out and around the edges of fields and forests. His quiet deepened. This time, we searched the wild ditches, the untilled edges, the grassy knolls, looking for the hidden, for those elusive, mottled and pitted umami of the fungal world. Morels. He drove slowly, speaking only now and then, *Sometimes they grow here but not every year*, steering down the two-track, watching the short grasses on the edge of the field—*They hide in there.* He nearly whispered, as though they were creatures he could frighten away.

Their growth was always the surprise crop. If my brothers were taming the gods of the fields, here was a crop that resisted all the manipulation and machinations of human control. Here, a hunt and chance pick, a search and fail, a crop never planted, only discovered. From his open window, his eyes trained, he could spot them. Unbelievable, what he saw in his quiet observations. Perhaps it was the color blindness that allowed him to pick out shapes the rest of us missed. He had worked in WWII in what he called sniper spotting. He was good at it because he was not misled by color. He understood and identified objects by shape and textures instead. He will not talk about this; we know it only through hearsay and mystery.

So it was no surprise he spotted morels that I could not see at all.

He pointed for me. *My legs is tired*, he said; he'd already had two walks that day. I couldn't be sure he was telling the truth but I didn't much care. Somewhere in the grass, there were morels. Usually two or three only. Then back into that cab, to show him. *Good. Good.* Then he'd drive on.

Just north of the new pole buildings, on a fence line of poplar and fescue. He had pointed, but I couldn't see anything. For a moment, I thought he just wanted to stop, feel the air moving off this land, but when I hopped down from the truck, I saw what I had missed, dozens of rough cone shapes in the grass. A boon of them. He passed down his fertilizer cap. I picked them all, loaded in the bowl of that cap, and holding it by the duckbill, carried them back to him.

Well now, that's just dandy, he said. We grinned and sniffed the load. The light shone through the trees with the first spring days that would hold afternoon heat. The small crop glowed between us. He sat in the same silent pride he'd have held for a hundred ton of carrots, the way some farmers can maintain quiet in their success, the way some men never need to make a big deal out of any accomplishment. *Dandy*, he had said. That was real good. Maybe that was exceptional.

I fried up some at supper, but I took most of them home, froze part.

I didn't know he would die in two months. I didn't know it was the last time I would tour the farm with him, the last time we would be in the fields together. I didn't know it was the last time we would share that ritual of intimate ease, picking the green, hunting the fields. Sometimes the crop is memory, something hidden that you have to go back into time and pick. Sometimes the crop is the field itself, the living of those ditches and furrows.

After the shock of that call, the one that came two months later, I had to cast back, when had I seen him last? I found the moment rising like an irregular shape, a small harvest: it was spring, morel season, the crop that cannot be predicted, cannot be planned. The crop that hides at the end of the long fields.

The Blue

In the end, the creatures found it. They were the ones who knew what to do.

A couple decades ago my dear friend Mimi gave me a blue sweater. Not just any blue sweater, but one that had been knitted by her mother in Denmark. When her mother died, Mimi—who had gone to be with her—brought it back, and gave it to me. Open stitches, soft wool, equally soft shape—that loose pullover style meant for cuddling. And blue, a stunning, singing, deep song. Winter blue, dark sapphire blue, ah yes, Scandinavian blue.

I cherished the sweater. Each winter, I anticipated pulling it out of storage on the coldest mornings of our Michigan darkness. The warmth and color never faded; I could rely on it when things were unreliable. When I wore it, I always looked to the sky for a match, and found it finally in those clear-hued December evenings. That blue, strongest just before real dark fell.

The winter after I lost my father, I pulled the sweater off the shelf, shook it out, and was shocked and saddened to find moths had invaded. A handful of holes blinked in the weave. I mended it and wore it two more winters, but the yarn had weakened. More holes laced the knit. The sweater was done. Was that the spring I lost two more friends: one, heart attack; another, cerebral hemorrhage?

Finally, I took the blue into my arms, apologized to Mimi's mother, and threw it over the back clothesline hoping maybe the Waxwings would raid it; they like string and single strands of stuff. That *sacre bleu* hung all summer and early fall; no waxwings. The blue never faded, and with the first snows, it shone against the white of a thin new snow. I looked at it every morning I came to the porch, coffee in hand. Its shabby obstinacy drew my eyes.

I missed my father, my friends, more than I could say.

One day, the sweater disappeared. Gone. I can't articulate the contradictions I felt. Relief—some thing had taken it at last, and loss—all over again. That swath of ultramarine had hung like a spirit friendship with a woman I never knew, but I did know because of her skill and her daughter's gift. It also stood for my lost friends. Their spirits, that blue. I studied the ground under the clothesline, scuffed through the garden, searching for the remnants. Nothing.

Later, while packing up the garden one rough-winded day, I caught sight of a blue strand. It led under the woodshed. When I dislodged an old clay pot, there, a blue tangle woven with dry leaves in a nest where a mouse or vole had kept warm. All through late fall, I found traces, a strand hooked in the wood pile, a filament caught in the window box, and once, what might have been a clump in a tree. A squirrels' nest woven blue into the cross-hatch of high-tree debris?

They were using it, but I had not seen. Like grief I suppose, eventually we weave it in, but invisibly.

Around Thanksgiving, I found what remained of the sweater in the ravine below our house. Just tatters, but identifiable. It had finally faded to the tired blue after storm. What remained fell apart in my hands; those warm mornings frayed in my fingertips. I stood on the hillside, amazed. Here was a piece of sky, now of earth, scattered by chance winds and the choices of wild creatures. What was lost? Warmth, color, connection? What was gained? A nest, a coil of new meaning, some organic fiber woven into a home. I leave it there in the wild. I'm a fool for loss, but there's also beauty: sky on a partly sunny morning, light warming the winter garden, the ecology of being human with mouse, squirrel, sweater and winter.

That deep blue dusk as dark comes on.

It's not done yet. Nearing Solstice, as we move wood out of the woodshed, I discover a phoebe nest in the eaves. Left from summer. When I pull it down to check if the nest had been a success, there, a thin filament of blue looping in the grassy bowl of emptiness. All through our woods, that blue has been knitted a second time. This is how creatures do it, making useful those faded but enduring fibers. Here, just before the year turns, I tug a single-strand from spiraled grasses. I let it catch the wind. Here's what matters, the way this cast-off never fully decays, the way friendship lives on in memory, and then becomes sacred in its adaptive use—blue thread still linking an endless sky to a battered but vital earth.

Acknowledgments

Earlier versions of the following first appeared in *Traverse, Up North Media* under the features "Reflections on Home" or "Up in Michigan":

"Sacred Fear"; "Beach Glass"; "Window Pains"; "Elegy for a Hardware Store"; "Tree Cutting"; "A Map of Hands (Breaking the Green)"; "The Secret Place"; "Stone Courtesy (A Stone from a Wilder Season)"; "In these Walls (Within these Walls)"; "Winter House"; "When Eden Shifts"; "Smudge (Orchard Smoke)"; "Splitting Wood"; "Vulnerability (Living it Up)"; "Hot Cup of Winter"; "Fallings"; "The Blue"; "Wishbones and Scars"; "Ghost Orchard"; "Kuieren (Coiyurra)"; "The Tree Cutting"; "Old Beams (What the Beams Said)"; "In Search of a Small Plan"; "October"

The following appeared in the *Glen Arbor Sun* and *Michigan Council for the Humanities* publications:

"Sweet Cider"; "Three Tales: Dune Meditations"

Anne-Marie Oomen is the author of *As Long as I Know You: The Mom Book* (2022), which won AWP's Sue William Silverman Nonfiction Award and a Michigan Notable Book Award. Her other titles include *The Lake Michigan Mermaid* (with Linda Nemec Foster, Michigan Notable Book 2019); *Love, Sex and 4-H* (2015); *Pulling Down the Barn* (2004) and *House of Fields* (2006) (Michigan Notable Books); *An American Map: Essays* (2010); and a collection of poetry, *Uncoded Woman* (2006).

She edited *Elemental: A Collection of Michigan Nonfiction* (Michigan Notable Book 2018), and *Looking Over My Shoulder: Reflections on the Twentieth Century* (2000). She is founding editor of *Dunes Review*, former president of Michigan Writers, Inc., and instructor at Solstice MFA in Creative Writing at Lasell University (MA) and at Interlochen College of Creative Arts.

She and her husband, David Early, built their own home on wild acreage near Empire, Michigan, and their beloved Lake Michigan.